The Canvas of My Soul

Robert Malouf

Cyberwit.net
HIG 45 Kaushambi Kunj, Kalindipuram
Allahabad - 211011 (U.P.) India
http://www.cyberwit.net
Tel: +(91) 9415091004
E-mail: info@cyberwit.net

Printed at Repro.

Contents

A Child's Plea

In the still of night,
I seemed to hear a child's haunting, chilling plea,
A plea echoed by untold millions of the world's children
Living in fear, abject poverty and hopelessness:

Childhood,
Where have you fled?
What of the joyful,
Smiling days
And happy moments promised,
The sunlit playgrounds
And beckoning, flowering fields?

Where is the glee and laughter
Of life's early years,
The bright, sunny days
Of frolic and play?
The safe embrace
Of peaceful night?

Childhood,
Tell me true!
What of family and friends,
Teachers and loved ones?
Are these my birthright,
The God-given right
Of every child?
If this be so,
Then why

Are emptiness and sadness
My only family,
Aloneness and loneliness,
My true, boon companions!

Today,
Amidst blowing travail and raging war,
Famine and pain,
Tragedy and blight,
I stretch my hand,
Ever hopeful
For some small act of kindness,
Some small morsel,
Even a handful of flour,
But to what avail?
It holds but empty promises,
The flight of hope and relief.

These effusions of my soul,
Perhaps unwelcome and assuredly brief –
A sad cry from the heart
Tempered only by my days of plight and grief –
Have left me tired and weary,
Though much is left to say,
But, that will be for some other time,
Some other day,
Should breath and voice,
The will to live,
The strength to pray,
Still be mine!

A Seed Is Planted

In Nature's garden
A seed is planted.
Seasons pass,
A rose comes forth,
Unfolds,
Its petals lovely
Or not,
Fragrant
Or not,
But always
Fully exposed.

With time petals fall,
Fragrant
Or not,
Gathered for perfume
Or not,
To adorn neck and bosom
Or not,

In the garden of humanity,
Each soul,
A seed of possibilities,
Is planted
To grow, develop,
Unfold its petals even as the rose.

With the passing of seasons,
Our petals fall,

Are gathered
Or not,
Valued
Or not
Remembered
Or not.

With each breath,
Each thought and act,
We unfold.
When seasons end
And petals fall,
May they be fragrant,
Lovingly gathered,
Remembered,
Cherished.

If not,
Then,
For what the planting?

All That Life and Nature Have to Teach

How can the lowly drop
Comprehend the surging sea
Or the streambed
Conceive the depths of the ocean floor?

How can the rising dawn
Understand the setting of the sun
Or the crescent moon
Grasp the brilliance of day?

How can the grain of sand
Envision the endless shore
Or the shell
Describe the lustre of the pearl?

How can the thorn
Savor the fragrance of the rose
Or prickly thistle
Appreciate the delicate beauty of the orchid?

How can the tiny seed
Grasp the tall and mighty tree
Or prairie grass
Conceive of mountain forests, deep ravines?

How can the gnat
Understand the flight of the eagle
Or the butterfly
Perceive the blazing speed of the falcon?

If such limitations be true,
Then how can the finite
Comprehend the infinite
Or the created
Understand the Uncreated?

How can the human spirit
Comprehend the Eternal Mystery
Or the mind
Grasp the Origin of creation?

All created things
Bear missives of mystery to unravel,
Spiritual realities to unfold.
Should truth and the sublime
Be our quest,
Then with hearts pure,
Sight and hearing sanctified,
May the journey begin,
That the garden of our hearts
Bloom in flowering wisdom
And fragrant understanding,
And the rose-covered trellises of the spirit
Perfume meaning and purpose,
Joy and contentment,
For then,
In the bursting light of a new dawn
All that life and Nature have to teach
Will be within our grasp,
Well within our reach.

Always the Light!

Never the diamond,
Though precious it may be –
Always the light!
Never the beauty of the rose,
Though lovely it may be –
Always the fragrance!
Never the appearance –
Always the reality!

Never the ruby,
Though exquisite it may be –
Always the light!
Never the bright form of hyacinth,
Though comely it may be –
Always the fragrance!
Never the appearance –
Always the reality!

Never the emerald,
Though a rare beauty it may be –
Always the light!
Never the visage of gardenia,
Though welcoming it may be –
Always the fragrance!
Never the appearance –
Always the reality!

Never the sapphire,
Though unrivaled it may be –

Always the light!
Never the bell shape of the lily,
Though intriguing it may be –
Always the fragrance!
Never the appearance –
Always the reality!

Never the pearl,
Though matchless it may be –
Always the light!
Never the charm of jasmine,
Though enticing It may be –
Always the fragrance!
Never the appearance –
Always the reality!

Never the gem –
Always the light!
Never the form –
Always the fragrance!
Never the grand illusions of life –
Always the real, the eternal, the essence –
Therein joy and wonder,
Happiness and contentment,
Dwell, live long, rejoice and flourish,
Never to die!

Appearances

Mother of pearl,
Gift giver of the sea,
I see your gleaming, lustrous gem!

Rose, ruby red,
How precious, breathtaking, your ruby petals,
How intoxicating your timeless, prized perfume!

Songbirds plump of breast, nesting high,
I hear your sweet songs, warbling melodies,
The compositions you so artfully trill!

Eagle, proud and strong, master of the sky,
How high your flight, majestic your form,
How keen your eye, how swift your capture of unsuspecting
prey!

Windflowers,
I see your bursting colors, blooms of spring,
Your playful swaying in the springtime breeze, wistful smiles
aglow in sunlight!

Appearances,
No matter their loveliness or how highly they are prized,
Are fleeting, ephemeral.
Like raindrops falling from the sky
Or autumn snow upon warm ground,
They last but for a time,
A seeming twinkling of the eye,

As do fallen leaves and lifeless blooms
Blown far and wide by pitiless winds, racing gales,
Unyielding, unrelenting time!
Human life, too, lingers but briefly
And then, like the seasons,
Moves on!

Archer of Heavenly Light and Love

Archer of heavenly light and love,
Hear our plea!
Hesitate not!
Draw hard your bow of luminous splendor
From the realm of transcendent glory,
Then fling your arrow of effulgent enlightenment
And penetrating spirituality
Into the heart of mankind,
That it be renewed,
Revived,
Beat in luminous love,
Throb in resplendent tranquility.

And should the heart of mankind
Not respond,
O great Archer,
Respite not!
Hurl your arrows of blazing light and love
Into the soul of a benighted,
Troubled humanity,
That it become illumined,
Shine as the Sun,
Its rays illuminating all peoples
With love, peace, goodwill and cheer.

Archer of the Divine,
How pervasive the darkness!
How bleak the dark night of unrest,
Ubiquitous injustice!
All peoples yearn,

Knowingly or unknowingly,
For the arrows you fling!
Spare no effort!
Rush forth!
Draw your bow!
Then illuminate
With blazing arrows of flaming glory
Mortal skies with brilliant hopes and sunlit dreams,
Aspirations that rise as the dawn,
Traverse the heavens of oneness and fellowship
As the Sun, orb of glory, traverses the sky,
That they radiate harmony and contentment,
Illumine every heart
With shining joy, glowing happiness.

O great Archer of heavenly light
And transformative, glorious love!
Draw your bow!
Fling your arrows!
Time is short
And there is no time to lose,
For many the heart
Awaiting your arrows of luminous unity,
Splendid justice,
Glorious love and wisdom!
Disappoint us not,
This we ask,
For if not you,
O Archer of the Divine,
Who then,
Will illuminate humanity's heart,
Brighten its soul,
Dispel the dark night of a divided world,
Illumine an estranged, struggling humanity!

As Swallows Fly

Love,
Fly to me
As swallows fly to Capistrano,
Faithfully, without fail!
Make haste,
Lest I waste away,
For my heart,
Eager, anxious,
Needs you so!

Soar the heavens!
Dance the sailing winds
If it please you!
But forget me not,
For I patiently await
The healing balm
Of your shining visage,
The encouragement
Of your sweet, warm embrace.

Romance the moonlight!
Play among the clouds,
Tease them if you must!
Bid them well,
Friendly winds and bellies full
That bountiful spring showers fall
And tree and flower
Hail their fidelity,
Their precious, life-giving drops.

But, then,
Come to me!
It is you I long for!
You I hope for!
You I pray to be
My bosom,
Eternal companion!

Should you encounter
Birds flying high
Or eagles,
Majestic masters of the heavens,
Chasing the horizon,
Fly with them!
For,
They, too,
Long for you,
Seek your company,
Your wise counsel,
The grandiose sweep
Of your flight.

And should angels,
Pure and holy,
Beauteous beyond word,
Illumined as the summer sky
And brilliant as softly flowing rivers of light,
Descend from realms unseen,
Promised, ethereal,
Seek your company,
By all means,
Consort with them!
Dance with them!

Assure them of your love,
Your undying gifts!

But,
O beloved of my soul!
My heart's desire!
In the end,
Deny me not!
Fly to me!
For I am yours
And without you
My heart
Is but throbbing dust;
My being
A temple without spirit;
My dreams and hopes,
Heavens searching for sun and moon,
Starry nights.

Without you,
And to this
My entire reality does testify,
I will remain but an empty shell
In search of its pearl;
A body bent in sorrow
Wandering aimlessly hill and vale,
Empty and forlorn
In its quest for love –
The mystic flame
That alone
Can light the lamp
Of my soul.

As Waves Move to the Shore

As waves move to the shore,
So do Thy lovers move to Thee.

As winds blow through the trees,
So it is with winds of love that move through the heart,
Enraptured, enamored of Thee.

As the Sun rises with the morn,
So does the Sun of Truth rise and shine
In the souls of those who turn to Thee.

As the stars shine,
So do the stars of wonderment
In the grand,
Incomparable firmament of love
And the splendrous orbs of adoration
In the supernal heavens of the spirit
Shine in the realities
Of those whose hearts,
Like a mirror
Longing for the light,
Reflect Thee.

Behold Me!

I thought I heard creation,
My soul awed,
Enamored of her beauty
And riding upon her winds,
Call to me in melodies
Played from robins' nests
And rustling leaves,
Murmuring brooks
And tonal, mountain streams,
"Behold me!".

With this,
My eyes,
Well nigh blinded
By her beauteous countenance,
Shining radiance,
And swooning away
In the sunlight of her dazzling charm,
Enchanting demeanor,
Beheld what only the heart dare see,
The soul dare contemplate.

Immersed in the glory
Of so beauteous a visage,
I humbled myself before her,
Wept silently
At what she let me see of her mystery,
Her tales of truth
Written by the Pen Of the Divine.

Daring to look again,
I beheld her gaze,
And lo,
She beckoned me to her warm embrace,
The rapturous heaving of her full bosom,
Her nurturing breast.
There she unfolded before eye and heart
The hidden mysteries of life and love,
The verdancy of spring,
The fragrance of the rose.

Heart and soul enthralled,
Wrapt in astonishment
And breathless before her,
She patiently awaited my glance,
My insatiable, passionate desire for more.
With this,
She unraveled riddles of time and space,
Revelation, the Prophets.
Then,
Beseeching her
With an audacity I could not suppress,
My soul cried out,
"Unfold, O beauteous maiden!
Still more!
For the intoxication of your presence
Has left the cup of my being
Craving your sweet wine,
The inebriating magnificence
You unfold."

With this,
She revealed a fleeting glimpse

Of the matchless beauty and empowering unity
Destined for humanity,
The luminous gems and treasures of the soul,
The nobility of the human spirit,
Its capacity to love,
Forgive, persevere.

I thought I heard her,
Once again,
Call to me,
To draw nigh,
To hear her whisper
Wonders to waft across the ages,
Enlighten the seeking heart,
The pure in spirit.
These thrilled me,
Even as moon and stars thrill the night,
As dawn thrills the morn.

Heart and soul afire,
Burning to ash idle fancy,
Igniting truths unread,
And unable to bear more,
I awakened from her rhapsodic call
Desirous to praise her beauty,
Glorify her essence in word and rhyme
With melodies from the heart
And harmonies of the soul,
That I might pen but a glance
Of her wondrous beauty,
The mystique of her countenance,
Though such a visage,
Breathtaking,

Timeless,
Born of Mystery,
The breath of the Divine,
Is, and this I know,
Except by the Pen of the Beloved,
Impossible to write.

Blackbird

Blackbird,
Dark night of my soul,
Fly away!
Leave nest and bough and branch
To return no more,
For I hear the cry of howling gales
Calling you to the far-off, desolate skies of oblivion
Beyond the horizon of remembrance,
There to nest on barren branches
Deep within the forest of the forgotten.

Blackbird,
The shining morn of Truth has dawned!
The croaking of the raven and cawing of the crow,
Harsh and hard to bear,
Are no longer welcome,
For the sweet songs of the Nightingale of Love
Call to me in gleaming melodies of light,
Each rapturous note warbled
From high atop the Tree of Life.

Blackbird,
Make way!
For the Nightingale calls,
And I,
Enamored of its song,
And with heart enchanted and soul enthralled,
Wish naught but to listen!

Blazing Suns

Blazing suns,
Orbs of glorious light
Illuminating the heavens,
Blaze forth!
Tell the tale you tell so well,
Of blazing love and flaming truth
To illumine the heart,
Enthrall the soul.

Black of night,
Lover of splendor,
Your one true beloved,
And canvas of space and time,
Would that hearts dark,
Souls a starless night,
Be as you are,
A resplendent canvas
Adorned in splendrous hues
Of divine light.

Blazing suns of love –
Hearts pure and undefiled
Radiating love in rapturous waves
Of gleaming affection –
Shine forth on the canvas of the seeking heart
In the placeless heavens of the soul,
That through you peoples be illumined,
Mind and thought be enlightened,
And mankind find its way in this pitch dark night

Guided by the illuminating, eternal,
Transforming splendor
Of the light
Of love.

Breathtaking Winds

Breathtaking winds,
Lift me high!
Fling me beyond sky and moon
That I feel alive,
Rejoice within!
If this be too much to ask,
Then unfold my inner being
As clouds unfold the rain,
That heavenly, spiritual rains
Drench me, revive me,
Vivify the life of the spirit!
And if this still be too much to ask,
Then unfold within my heart
The sweet savors of heavenly hyacinth
That waft upon your winds
Sacred perfumes of wonderment and mystery
That enchant, intoxicate,
Create anew.

Then,
If it be not too much to ask,
Blow across
The canyons of my soul,
Its deep ravines and dry riverbeds,
That these be transformed into hills and valleys
Of flowering love and goodness,
Flowing rivers and streams watering thirsty lands
With kindliness and goodwill.

Breathtaking winds,
Be not shy!
Tell me,
From where do you blow?
From what heaven do you descend?
Might it be the holy realm
Of eternal truths and sacred mysteries?
Or perhaps veiled and hidden realms
Adorned in light so beauteous
As to illuminate body and soul
With peace and contentment,
Tranquility and composure?

Or perhaps,
It is from the All-Glorious Beloved
That you descend,
His sweet, life-giving breath
Empowering your mighty winds
Of truth and love
That transform the earthly
Into the angelic,
The sinful into the righteous,
The hard of heart and dead of spirit
Into a living being,
Godly, grateful, fulfilled.

Whatever your origin,
The source of your ethereal,
Transforming winds,
Breathe your mystic breeze
Deep into my soul!
Flow through my being
Even as a mighty river

Vivifying heart and soul,
That I be spiritually alive
While yet there is time!

Breathtaking winds,
Stop not with me!
Blow your transcendent zephyrs
Across the soul and within the spirit
Of an ailing mankind,
For humanity calls to you,
Beseeches you,
That your wafting joy and love,
Fragrant meaning and truth,
Revive its soul, purify its heart!
Give it strength to breathe
Your mighty rejuvenating breaths
Of justice and oneness,
Love of all peoples,
Peace and prosperity!

Blessed winds,
Humanity is gasping for air,
Struggling for its life,
Its heart nigh unable to beat!
Come forth!
Revive its soul!
Transform its character!
And if it be not you,
O breath of God,
Who, then,
Is able to save it!

Bridge to Eternity

Bridge to Eternity,
Sacred crossing of longing lovers
To the ethereal realms of the Divine Beloved,
My soul seeks your ancient promise,
Infinite, soul-stirring heights,
That I might find my way
To the holy court of the Loved One,
Behold the wonders of His countenance,
The beauty of His visage,
Find rapturous intoxication from the ancient casks
Of His vintage ruby Wine
Poured letter by letter, word by word
And imbibed from the sublime chalice
Of transformative Revelation,
Wonderment and mystery.

Bridge to the Eternal,
I long for the mystic poems He writes,
The heavenly lessons He teaches,
The truths He unfolds petal by petal
In the rose garden of His wondrous, radiant heart.
They say reality,
In rapture and ecstasy,
Circle round His holy Presence
As the lovestruck nightingale,
Enamored warbler of love,
Circles about the rose,
Swoons away from its perfumed charm,
And as the moth of undying devotion,

Oblivious to rest and sleep,
Circles round the lighted torch of eternal love,
An undying lesson to the godly and the seeker,
Those with eyes to see and ears to hear.

They say
He is even as the Sun
But brighter still,
Far more glorious,
That God-intoxicated lovers circle about His abode,
How much more His holy Presence,
Even as Moon and Earth circle the Sun.
They say His voice is the voice of God,
His truth the truth of God,
His Revelation revealed at the command of God.
They say He transforms the heart, purifies the soul,
And burns to ash the confusion of mind and spirit
With but a loving glance, the wave of His hand,
The sweetness of His smile.

I have heard it said
He revives the dead,
Makes whole the sick,
Gives balm to the suffering
With His command,
"Arise! Take up thy soul! For this is the promised hour,
The promised Day of God!",
That His wise and loving exhortations ride the holy winds
That blow freely as the summer wind
Across and through,
The sacred valleys of His soul
And the perfumed garden of His heart.
They say the merest stroke of His pen

On the tablet of the heart
Bestows life everlasting, joy and gladness,
And that His Holy Word creates souls anew,
Resurrects, brings to life, the fallen and the forlorn,
The wayward and the lost.

Bridge to Eternity,
You call to me!
I hear your sweet voice,
Your thundering call to arise,
Make haste, struggle,
Be as you were created to be!
It is all this,
O Bridge to Eternity,
That I hear in your call!
All this
That resonates in my soul!

Bridge to the Eternal Beloved,
I have walked through misty fog and bitter cold,
The dark of night, lonely canyons of the heart,
Stony paths of the soul.
From these I am weary, lost and tired,
Unwilling to tread, even one day more,
These paths of gloom.

Bridge of Eternity,
Your splendid, heavenly heights,
Alone, I wish to walk,
But, alas, you must reveal yourself,
Bid me enter, let me pass,
That my soul find meaning and truth,
Purpose and love, hopes and dreams,

And the dying embers of my spirit,
Well nigh spent,
Be ignited by the mystic fire of His love
Deep within me,
Set ablaze my soul,
Recreate, warm and illumine
The barren wasteland
And cold, forsaken ground
Of what is left of me!

Budding Rose in the Burgeoning Bloom of Spring

Budding rose
In the burgeoning bloom of spring,
What romantic tales have you to tell
Of love and lovers long ago,
Dancing damsels
And swooning suitors?

What mysteries do you reveal
With every unfolding petal?
What perfume of ages past,
Truths eternal, never lost,
Do you waft to passing winds,
The softly blowing zephyrs of spring?

Budding rose,
What secrets of life and love,
Meaning and purpose,
Have you to reveal
With the dawning light of each new day?
Is it that ancient wisdom lives on,
Inviolable, unassailable,
Unaffected by time,
Informing realities in this Day of Days?

Or is it that a rose
Of incomparable beauty and fragrance
Has begun to bloom, captivate hearts,
Transform the souls of of all mankind?

If this be true,
Then from what garden does this rose bloom,
How will I know it,
Where can it be found?

Upon blowing winds
Of a spiritual reawakening
I hear a soft and gentle call
To enlightenment, love and peace,
Beauty and rapture,
And savor a sweet, alluring perfume
That bids me
Enter the rose garden of the heart,
The innermost sanctuary of the soul,
Walk its trellised avenues,
Breathe its air,
Delight in its sumptuous,
Splendid beauty.

Enraptured,
Overcome with wonder
And intoxicated
By a spiritual redolence
I can not describe,
I enter,
Exhilarated,
Filled with wonder,
For therein I behold
A rose of matchless beauty,
Of heavenly fragrance, exquisite form,
Each breathtaking petal
Perfumed in spirituality,
Redolence sublime,
Lessons of the heart.

Deep within,
Where the sacred longs to dwell
And the mighty sea
Of search and hope surges
Beckoning me ride its billowing waves,
Where heavens of reunion
Are illumined by the brilliant stars
Of what one can be,
And white-hot bolts of longing
Blaze across its outspread skies,
I bear witness
To the supernal sanctity before me,
To transforming, creative power,
Contentment and joy,
For I stand,
Humbled, as naught,
Enthralled,
Before magnificence and glory,
Godliness and truth,
The eternal, ever-beauteous
Rose of Love.

Canvas of My Soul

O canvas of my soul,
Have I painted you vivid and bright
With colors joyous, wondrous,
That revive,
Portray the luminous light of love
In brilliant hues
Of a worthy life?

And what of my brush,
The strokes I ply?
Are they strong and true,
Wielded with wisdom and care,
Or have I impatiently, hurriedly,
Brushed colors dim and dark upon you,
Causing you sadness,
Disappointment and despair?

From deep within,
Where truth lives
And judgment speaks,
Where happiness rejoices
And grief is stricken,
Comes the reply:
Arise with courage, unafraid,
Then ask what you will
Of heart and conscience,
For therein,
Alone,
Your answer lies.

Should the response displease or sadden,
Take up the brush and paint anew
From the all-forgiving palette
Of a contrite, sincere heart
With strokes of love,
Colors vivid and bright
That warm the heart,
Illumine the spirit.

Should this you do,
The canvas of your soul
Will come alive in hues of peace and joy,
Brilliant light and glorious warmth.
Its idyllic scenes of quiet tranquility
And radiant beauty,
With its lush, green fields of encouragement,
Meadows of flowering kindliness and compassion,
And blue skies of contentment,
Will brighten the hearts
And refresh the canvas
Of those you love,
Those you meet,
Those who,
Spiritual artists at heart,
Yearn and strive to paint anew,
With the brush of pure intention
And a palette of heavenly hues,
The God-given gift
Of the ethereal
Canvas of the soul.

Come to Me!

I hear the call of the wind
As it blows through my soul, tantalizes my spirit –
Come fly with me!

I hear the call of the stars
As they sparkle, paint in light the nighttime sky –
Shine for me!

I hear the call of playful, dancing leaves –
Dance and rustle in the fragrant winds of love with me!

I hear the call of blossoming springtime blooms –
Burst into heavenly colors of joy and happiness for me!

I hear the call of the sea –
Dive deep for the pearls of mystery latent deep within thee!

I hear the call of Nature's songs,
Melodious, sweet, from the warbling of songbirds –
Sing with me!

I hear the call of time,
How quickly I pass! How fleeting this earthly life! –
Treasure me!

I hear the call of mountains, hilltops high –
Stand firm, unwavering as the Alps,
On the path to the Beloved!

I hear the mystic call of the Unseen –
Come to me, O thou who art my lover!
Make haste!
Wing thy flight to the realm of the All-Glorious!

All things call to me!
In them
I hear the call of the Beloved!
In them
I hear what my ardent soul,
My yearning spirit,
Alone,
Do seek!

Communion With the Beloved

In moments of deep reflection
I thought I heard Him say:

Clear away thy false imaginings
And reflect,
Reality is within thee!

Clear away thy freighted chains
And arise,
Arising is within thee!

Clear away thy dross
And fly,
Flight is within thee!

Clear away thy vain desires
And soar,
Soaring is within thee!

Clear away thy earthly attachments,
To all that is worldly,
For heaven is within thee!

Clear away all that is not of Me
That you may find Me,
For I am,
And forever will be,
Within thee!

Dusk Till Dawn

Dusk till dawn,
I hear her cry,
Her falling tears.

Dusk till dawn,
Stars shine,
Gleaming pearls across the sky,
And moonglow,
Ancient lamp of night,
Strives to brighten her cheek
With beaming rays of hope and solace.
Still, I hear her lamentation,
Her elegy of sorrow,
The outpouring of her heart.

Dusk till dawn,
Quiet and still,
She patiently endures
Separation from her beloved,
His luminous presence,
Inimitable, glorious,
A separation she alone
Must bear.

Dusk till dawn,
She patiently awaits his return,
The warmth of his smile,
The radiance of his love,
His unfailing fidelity,

The flourish
Of life and love and joy
He brings.

Dusk till dawn,
Faithful, true,
She awaits her beloved,
The tenderness of his touch,
The matchless splendor
He breathes deep into her bosom.

Dusk till dawn,
Earth,
Fair maiden that she is,
Awaits the rising Sun,
Her one, true beloved,
Orb of magnificence
Who, alone,
Warms her,
Causes her trees to grow,
Fruits to ripen,
Her flowers to blossom and bloom,
Her birds to sing.

Wrapped in love,
Bound by space and time,
Lovers to the end,
They give birth to life,
Rivers that flow,
Seas that rise and surge,
Winds that blow.
Through them,
Their undying devotion,

Fealty that knows no end,
Swallows fly and songbirds sing,
Nightingales swoon away
Before the rose,
Butterflies flutter,
Bees build their hives.

Dusk till dawn
Earth awaits her beloved.
Dawn to dusk
She celebrates the miracle of life.

From Earth and Sun
There is much to learn;
Tales of hope, stories of dreams
To ponder, unravel;
Eternal truths of love and faithfulness,
Fortitude and patience
To grasp, understand;
Mystic riddles
Awaiting the seeking soul
To explore,
Unfold,
Plant with love
In the eternal garden
Of the heart.

Ecstasy

Ecstasy,
Is that you at the portal
Of my heart,
Pulsating
Chamber to chamber,
Exciting the crimson rivers
That flow therein?

It must be so,
For who else
Dare dance in verse,
In rhythm and rhyme,
Rejoice as wafting springtide zephyrs
Perfumed in jasmine and rose,
Shine like sun and moon,
Nay! All the heavens
Within each line!

Ecstasy,
From me,
You can neither hide nor flee!
For I have found the hidden treasures,
The priceless gems of truth
Wherein you dwell,
The mystic heavens of ethereal beauty you fly,
The Paradise you call home!

Ecstasy,
Let us rejoice,

Make merry as one,
Dance the floor of wonderment as one,
Soar the supernal skies of purity and holiness as one,
For you are mine and I am yours,
And within the exalted Paradise of Revelation,
Forevermore,
And at His pleasure,
May we be
As one!

Fall

Fall,
Faithful season
Of red and yellow, orange and gold,
With the passing of summer
You unfailingly visit our lives,
Mindful of Mother Nature's
Ancient clockworks
Crafted by the hands of time!

How unwavering you are!
You are like the sun
That rises from the east with the break of day,
Commands the sky dawn to dusk
In glory and resplendence,
Lifegiver to all that moves,
All that lives.

You call to mind
The storied constellations
And scintillating stars
That,
With the setting of the sun in the westerly sky –
Its retreat of rest and repose –
Traverse the heavens by night,
Faithful to their duty, their sacred pledge,
To rise in splendor,
Bedazzle the black of night,
Beget mystery and wonder.

Fall,
The warp and woof
Of your warm colors and memorable beauty
Weave a rich tapestry worthy to ponder,
One that causes souls to reflect
On the grand flow of the seasons,
Praise your gusting winds and rustling compositions
Played in notes red and yellow, orange and gold
To delight the heart, captivate the mind,
Give rise to awe, abiding appreciation.

Fall,
How diligently you remind us
Of the seasons of life –
The springtime of youth with its blossoming joys
And flowering romance and love;
The fruitful summer years
Yielding succulent, sweet fruits of meaning and purpose
To nourish the heart, refresh the soul, serve others;
The surrender of summer to fall,
When October winds blow through leaves
Whispering stories old,
Tales untold;
The deep sleep of winter.

Fall,
Even as you are pleased with seasons past,
May we be pleased
With the blooms and blossoms of spring
That are ours alone,
The springtime breezes our hearts have wafted,
The summer fruits we have cultivated and grown,
The warm summer nights of our own making.

And may the autumn of our years
Be colored in hues of love and kindness,
Goodness and generosity, friendship and benevolence,
Even as your leaves,
Faithful to Mother Nature's decree,
Are colored in hues of warmth and beauty,
Fidelity, unerring wisdom.
May we learn,
As have you,
From the truths She speaks,
The mysteries She unfolds, lays bare before us,
The profound lessons She teaches so well!

Fall,
Ever remind us
Of the passing of time,
The inexorable flow of life's seasons
Year after year and without exception –
A lesson to ponder,
That our lives,
When last leaves of fall,
No longer to come again,
Be forever remembered
In the beauteous, warm colors
Of red and yellow, orange and gold,
A worthy tribute
To a life betokening
Beauty and warmth,
The gifts of fall.

Fallen Petals of Shiraz

*In honor and remembrance of ten women
hanged in a public square in Shiraz the summer of 18 June 1983.
Their crime was refusing to renounce their religious beliefs
that included justice for all, gender equality
and the oneness of humanity.*

From the rose garden of the Beloved,
Nurtured and warmed by rays of glory
Released from supernal realms of the the All-Glorious,
Came forth heavenly blooms of spiritual luminosity
Perfumed at the Command of God
And by His empowering Will
To gently waft sweet savors of godliness
Across the land of Persia
And flow,
A gentle summer breeze
Of equality and empowerment,
Through receptive hearts and enlightened minds,
That the splendorous fragrance
Of the Rose of Love
Perfume all lands,
All peoples.

From the rose garden of the Beloved
Each beauteous petal –
Faithful, spiritual, courageous,
A testimony to the purity of their lives,
The soaring loftiness of their ideals,
The unchallengeable strength of their character –

Was ruthlessly plucked from the godly bush
Of unfeigned devotion and selfless service
By the sullied and vile hands of hatred
To be immolated by harsh and searing winds
Of religious fanaticism
And tormenting storms of unyielding cruelty.
Though now their petals long fallen,
Still, their heavenly fragrance lives on,
Ever sweeter, more widely wafted
Than even that fateful day
When ten fair maidens,
Adorned petals of redolent godliness
And heavenly beauty,
Fell,
Perfuming realities with wonder,
Hearts with awe,
Womanhood with glory.

From the Hand of God
They came.
By the hand of wanton tyranny
They fell,
Each petal testifying to the power of truth,
The unstoppable,
Vital and essential contributions of women
Of every faith, color and clime.

Fallen petals of Shiraz,
Though challenged with injustice and inequality,
And now released from this mortal garden
To dwell in gardens of holiness,
Still, your redolence –
Spiritual, moral, intellectual –
Lives on,

Its fragrance too sweet,
Too commanding,
To be obscured or denied.

Beauteous petals
From the rose garden of the Beloved,
How spiritually glorious your end!
How godless,
How sharp the sword of fanaticism
Wielded against you!
How foolish, effete, that hateful blade!
How inspiring your story! –
Unforgettable!
Undying!
Undenied!

And in the Realm of Glory,
Sanctified Garden of Holy Rapture,
How you must shine,
Petal soft and pure, beauteous, angelic,
Humble before your Lord
In the rose garden of the All-Glorious,
Hallowed Sanctuary of Splendor.
And there,
From that immortal Garden,
May your deathless faith,
Dauntless courage and sacred sacrifice
Perfume and inspire
Every flower in the garden of humanity
With fragrances of love and oneness,
That each may bloom in peace and tranquility,
The God-given right and promised destiny
Of all mankind.

Flow Through Me!

River of love,
Flow through me!
As rushing mountain streams,
Unrestrained,
Trysting with light and wind,
Beckoned, drawn close
By Earth's molten depths,
Flow from on high.

Plunge then
Into the very heart of me,
The unexplored depths of my being,
Even as ardent seekers plunge the depths of truth
And springtime lovers plunge the seas of romance,
Undying affection, fealty,
There to flow in rippling,
Sacred streams of purifying waters,
That my soul be cleansed,
My spirit revived,
My true reality –
Joyous, caring, loving –
Be awakened,
Brought forth,
Made alive.

River of love –
Undefiled, selfless love –
River of hidden mysteries,
Untold riddles of the spirit,

Revealer of wisdom,
Begetter of understanding,
Rush through me
As light speeds through space and time!
Purge me,
That the coursing rivers of my soul,
Bank to bank,
Be watered,
Bathed in awe and wonder,
Made fresh and sweet
By your peerless essence,
Transcendent gifts!

Descending from on high,
Eternal, timeless,
And with the full force
Of your mighty, transforming powers,
Come down as rapturous,
Racing falls
Crashing hard and long
Upon my soul,
That I be showered in love,
Immersed in your inimitable,
Vitalizing waters.

River of love,
Ancient mystery that you are,
Take no rest!
Rush through soul and heart,
Tirelessly, relentlessly,
Again and again!
Engulf me!
Create me anew
And in your image!

Then,
Even as a quiet pond,
May I,
Enraptured, enthralled,
Filled with love,
Reflect upon your luminous,
Mystic waters,
Eternal delights,
And exhilarated, with firm resolve,
Muse long and deep to unravel even a few
Of your myriad gifts and graces,
Live even but one.

Fly for Me!

Mighty eagle,
Spread wide your strong, powerful wings,
Thrust hard, take flight,
Fly for me!
Let me see as you see,
For your sight is supreme,
And I have neither wind
Nor wing to lift me high,
Nor sight so keen.
Alas,
Mine is but to ponder and wonder
At your flight.

Great bird of the heavens,
Soar far and long for me,
For my feet, unlike yours,
Are bound to ground
And flight in skies above
Beyond my reach.
It is in you
That I wish to fly realms above,
In you
That I wish to fly skies so high.

Majestic bird of prey,
Undisputed master of the heavens,
Rise to heights beyond sight and ken,
Sierra and sequoia,
For therein

Is where the eagle of my soul
Yearns to fly,
Albeit in the supernal heavens
Of my soul,
Where wings to soar are strong,
Sight is keen,
And ethereal winds to lift me high
Blow long and true,
And, like eternity itself,
Ever without limit!

For Some, Tomorrow

For some,
Tomorrow,
For others,
Today.

For some,
A frown,
For others,
A smile.

For some,
Harsh words,
For others,
Words of encouragement.

For some,
A hand held close,
For others,
A helping hand.

For some,
Illusion,
For others,
Reality.

For some,
Willful blindness,
For others,
Keen insight.

For some,
Doubt,
For others,
Hope.

For some,
Frivolity and folly,
For others,
Purpose and meaning.

For some,
Discontent,
For others,
Contentment.

For some,
Divisiveness,
For others,
Unity.

For some,
Cruelty,
For others,
Kindness.

For some,
Injustice,
For others,
Justice.

For some,
Worldliness,
For others,
Godliness.

For some,
Hate,
For others,
Love.

For all peoples,
So many choices,
For each one,
The power to choose.

Forests of Green

Forests of green,
Testimony to beauty, resilience,
Wondrous harmony,
Strength to withstand the ages,
How is it that you dwell in peace,
Each tree, one with another?

Is it
That you are connected root by root,
Content, even happy, to abide side by side?
Or is it your endless adoration of the Sun,
Your recognition of its magnificence,
Splendor and power?
I say this,
As I see you stretching long your branches
In humility and gratitude
To that peerless orb riding high the heavens,
Each branch invigorated, illumined,
By its warming light.

Perhaps,
It is that beauty,
When she heard your name,
Learned of your greatness
And visited you long ago,
Has, in the sweetest of voices,
Asked that each tree grow,
One with another,
In peace and tranquility

That she may,
Unrestrained and for all time,
Reveal her charms,
Spread wide the skirt of her adorning robes,
Unveil but a glimpse
Of her matchless countenance.

Or is it
That wind and rain,
Long time friends and great admirers,
Gifted you with their presence
That you heed their call,
Fulfill their every wish and whim?
Indeed,
We know how the wind loves your leaves,
To tease and jostle them about,
Hear them rustle the timeless tales they tell,
How the rain rushes to touch your canopy,
Water forest ground.

Or might it be
Your love for your diverse,
Colorful and feathered, flying friends
And the teeming, endless creatures,
Large and small,
That call you home,
Seek your protection,
Depend upon you for sustenance,
The tender nurture you provide?

Whatever the answer may be,
Stand fast!
Change not your ways!

For we are in dire need
Of the beauty and unity you teach,
The harmony and patience you exemplify,
And,
Bereft of this,
Dismayed and disillusioned,
We may well lose faith
In the unique beauty and organic oneness
The vast, diverse forests of humanity,
Now struggling,
Can, and must,
Attain.

From His Begetting Winds

When asked about the origins of creation,
A wise old sage offered this surprising reply:

From His begetting winds,
Vitalizing breaths of life,
Being, existence,
Surging seas of reality
And the billowing ocean of infinity,
Transcendence,
The human spirit.

From His palette,
Color and form,
Northern lights and rainbows –
Stunning, wondrous,
Thrilling to eye and heart –
The soul of mankind.

From the movement of His pen,
Scrolls of meaning and truth,
The book of creation,
Flowering fields of purpose,
Untold orbs of dazzling light,
Dazzling light within.

From the stroke of His brush,
Imagination, thought,
Outspread skies of comprehension,
Mystic heavens of faith and knowledge,

Reason, creativity,
Flowing streams of will and desire,
The resplendent dawn of wisdom
And shining morn of understanding.

From His love –
Brilliant rays of beauty and wonder
Unfolding in perfumed petals
Of contentment and joy
In the Springtime of the Divine –
The Rose of Love,
The greatest, most precious gift of all,
Impossible to fully grasp or deny,
Impossible not to ponder.

From Mystic Fire

A flirtation with brevity and rhyme

From Mystic Fire
My flaming soul has come,
Not from space and time,
These but the allure of shadowy illusion,
A portent to the wise, for the seeing a sign!

From Undying Love
My flaming heart was born,
That it live and love, learn and give,
Brightly shine, fly and soar!
And in realms celeste may I be granted this,
A heart pure, fully afire, unwilling to be quenched,
A thrall to the Loved One's beauty,
A thrall forevermore!

Not for ephemeral pursuits and worldly whims
These passing earthly days,
O how quickly they do pass!
But that the lines they pen
In deed and thought
And that cover every page,
Be inscribed upon the soul,
Their worth unfolded,
Their story told!

May the fire of love
Be a conflagration in my soul,

This my only wish,
That my heart,
A fiery torch aflame,
Please the Well-Beloved,
And in His Courtyard and His Presence,
His shining Countenance bid me linger,
Stay! Remain!

From Sun and Cloud

From Sun and cloud,
Mother Nature's warm bosom,
Light and rain, tender nurture,
The awakening of the seed,
Growth, development.

From the awakening of the seed,
The queenly rose,
Unfolding petals,
Color rich and vibrant.

From the rose,
Enchanting floral beauty,
From the passing of time,
Fallen petals to grace,
Enthrall the ground.

From fallen petals,
Perfume highly prized,
Fragrance sensuous, alluring,
To adorn in sweet savors
Neck and breast
Of maidens fair.

From seed and rose,
The perfumed tale
Of the journey of life,
Completion,

Mother Nature's wisdom,
Her telling light!

So, too,
Is the journey of the soul
From seed to ground –
Fallen petals and no more,
Or the sweet perfume of a life well-lived,
Its fragrant petals naught but love,
Its enchanting savors,
Spiritual delight!

From Feeble Heart

From feeble heart
My inspiration,

From feeble hand
The movement of my pen,

From feeble mind
The lines I write,

From feeble heart and feeble hand,
From feeble soul and feeble mind,
Feeble poetry to fill the page –
This my offering,
I can do no more.

But the ink of love
With which I write
Is as the expanse of the heavens,
As unstoppable, benevolent, raging falls
And fast-moving streams
Descending from mountaintops,
As fields of blooming hyacinth and rose,
As impassioned, relentless, springtime winds
That blow across and through
The lover's heart,
That blow strong and true,
Alive to love,
Alive to life,
Forevermore!

Though hand and heart be weak,
And soul and mind be feeble,
Still,
The ink is plentiful
And the ink is strong –
Who could wish for more!

From Whence This Love That Shines?

*Inspired by the luminous visage of a leaf blowing in the
springtime zephyrs of His love*

From whence this love that shines,
If not the luminous Lamp of Holiness
Illuminating the souls of angels?

From whence this love that gleams,
If not the Orb of Effulgence
Pulsating within breasts of holiness?

From whence this love that glows,
If not the lustrous Pearl of Love
Adorning the gemlike bosoms of damsels divine?

From whence this fragrance of love, so pure,
If not the sublime Essence of Love
Perfuming the hearts of godly maidens?

From whence this sweet savor of love,
If not the redolence of the Rose of Love
Wafting through the sanctuary of the soul?

From whence this heavenly joy of love,
If not the smiling lips of the Beloved
Creating ecstasy in the hearts of angels?

Unrestrained,
My soul cries out,

"From the Beloved,
Love and joy,
Gifts from Heaven's doors!
For seeking maidens of open heart,
The realm of angels, damsels of delight –
Mirrors of His love,
Lamps of His light!"

Gemlike Moment of the Soul

When the dawn of an open heart
Breaks as a summer morn
Across the horizon of the spirit,
And the sun of transcendence steadily rises
To blaze forth across the ecliptic of the soul
Spreading undulating rays of love and kindness
To warm the hearts of others,
Behold!
A gemlike moment of the soul!

When the full moon of justice
Reflects the effulgent light
Of fairness and fair-mindedness
And illuminates soul and heart and mind
To dispel the dark night of injustice
That it be no more,
Behold!
A gemlike moment of the heart!

When empowering,
Fragrant wafting breezes of generosity
Vitalize the chambers of the heart
And blow tirelessly across
The meadows and canyons of the soul,
Even as a zephyr of vernal thoughtfulness
To refresh and revive the poor bent low,
Behold!
A gemlike moment of the spirit!

When one's inmost being
Is illumined by the glorious Sun of Truth
Enthroned in the midmost heaven of the heart,
And the sacred profound of the spirit
Reflects dancing rays of happiness and joy,
Contentment and gratitude
To shine cheer and gladness upon souls dear and far,
Behold!
A gemlike moment of the heart!

When the seeker walks the spiritual path,
Heart yearning for holy, burgeoning blooms of the spirit
Adorned in unfolding petals of luminous purity
Perfumed in redolent sincerity, humility and selflessness,
And bounteous clouds of divine confirmation rain down
In salubrious, life-giving showers of certitude
Upon the garden of the heart,
Behold!
A gemlike moment of the spirit!

When all these come to pass,
Never to be lost
But honored and treasured,
Behold!
The gemlike life of the soul,
Eternal, transcendent,
Luminous!

I Have But One Heart

I have but one heart,
One mind,
One pen to write upon the page.

I have but one soul,
One love,
The love born of Thee.

I have but one dream,
One desire,
One hope,
These,
That I might fly
Where lovers fly and lovers tryst,
The trysting place
Of love of Thee!

I Seek Not

I seek not facts of Sun and Moon,
The vastness of space, the mysteries of the stars,
These are for brilliant minds of science,
Those with a passion for such things,
Not a humble intellect like mine.

I seek not the Himalayas,
To scale majestic mountain peaks,
Or even make my way across hill and vale,
These are for the fit and strong,
They are well-suited for such arduous pursuits.

I seek not worldly adventure,
To travel lands far, places magical and new,
These I leave for the wanderlust,
Those seeking the unknown,
The adventurous at heart.

I seek not the attractions of city life,
Buildings high, neon signs and lights,
Brightly lit boulevards and avenues wide,
These are better left for city dwellers,
Those who prefer such things.

No, for my part,
It is not the allure of the world I seek,
Or to travel and explore distant lands,
But the allure of the world within,
With its shining Sun and splendrous skies,

Where songbirds of the spirit
Warble melodious song
And eagles of the soul fly and soar
Lofty realms within,
Where winds of rapturous love blow
And nightingales of devotion,
Enthralled, wrapt in adoration,
Unwilling to depart the perfumed rose garden
Of the lover's heart,
Circle joyously, tirelessly,
The incomparable, sublime beauty
Of the soul's ethereal
Incomparable Rose.

In Her Womb[1]

In Her womb
A seed is planted,
Dwells in darkness,
Stretches to the light,

Grows,
Endures racing winds and pounding rain,
Frigid gales and chilling winter snow,
Searing days and frosty nights,
Soil parched,
Roots dry.

Mother Nature,
Also kind and loving,
Protective and caring,
Grants days of warming Sun,
Playful, frolicking clouds,
Gentle winds that caress, encourage,
Seasons mild,
Air sweet.

Through all these,
The seed becomes the rose,
The rose perfume,
The perfume a fragrance
Highly prized.

---

1. Mother Nature

As the seed,
We enter this world
Of gifts and throes,
But,
Unlike the seed,
The end is ours to choose –
Rose or thorn,
Prized perfume or prickly nuisance –
Unwanted,
Cast aside,
Its seasons wasted.

In the Garden of Life

In the garden of life,
Mother Nature birthed a seed
Destined to thrill sense and soul,
Inspire pen and poet, the hearts of lovers,
And named it "Rose."
In her bosom,
Warm and loving,
She nurtured it to maturity,
Until, at last, came forth,
Roses of magnificent beauty and fragrance.
For this,
The roses,
With humility and gratitude,
Gave praise for Sun and rain, soil and wind,
All that Mother Nature had bestowed.

Their exquisite redolence and beauty,
The softness of their petals,
Drew praise and appreciation
From blooms of spring and springtime showers,
Gentle zephyrs and wafting summer winds,
Songbird and butterfly,
The warbling of the nightingale,
All with eyes to see, heart to understand.

In the garden of life,
Too,
Came forth crows,
Croaking, envious,

Dismissive of their gifts of flight and brain
And jealous of the rose's beauty and fragrance,
Her charm and queenly qualities,
For she was, assuredly,
Alluring,
If not enchanting,
To the dwellers of that garden.

With time,
Crows pass,
Their croaking naught but silence,
For breath and life wing their flight,
As it is with all earthly things.
Their absence,
Unnoticed,
Perhaps even welcomed,
Is without mention or remorse,
Their end,
Unmarked ground.

With time,
Too,
Rose petals fall,
Their end to be gathered
By tender and loving hands,
Their fine perfume captured
To adorn breast and neck and cheek,
Hopes and dreams of maidens fair,
Their redolence prized across generations.

In the garden of humanity,
Some have chosen the way of the rose,
Others the way of the crow.

Should we but reflect we would see
That Mother Nature has lessons to teach,
Tales to tell,
And we,
For our part,
Have been given ears to hear.
How very important,
Then,
That we listen!

In the Lover's Heart

In the lover's heart,
Fiery flames of love
For the Loved One's beauty,
Flames to consume pride and prejudice,
Self and greed.

In the lover's soul,
Blazing fires
Of passionate devotion,
Searing heat to burn away,
Condemn,
The dross of spirit, earthly desire,
To the lifeless cold of oblivion,
Leaving in their stead
The Straight Path to His holy Presence
In the ethereal gardens of eternity.

In the lover's heart,
Now purified by longing love
And passionate devotion,
Flow crystal streams
Of wonderment and understanding
To refresh anemones of joy
And hyacinths of wisdom,
Revive tranquil ponds of contentment
And purling brooks of astonishment
That rush through heart and soul
To water again and again

And forevermore,
The fiery flames of love
For the Loved One's beauty.

In the Seeking Heart A Fire

In the seeking heart,
Sincere and true,
A fire,
From the fire the heat of love,
Heaven's kindly light.

From the heat of love,
The forging of the sword of truth,
From heaven's kindly light,
Wondrous waves of unfolding wisdom.

From the sword of truth
And wondrous waves of unfolding wisdom,
The slaying of self, inordinate desire,
Illumination of spirit,
Enlightenment of mind.

From the slaying of self, inordinate desire,
Illumination of spirit
And enlightenment of mind,
Spirituality, selflessness,
The outpouring of love,
Every good.

From all these,
A life rich and pure,
A generous, kindly spirit,
The shining light of meaning,
Life's purpose,

A shining jewel on the diadem
Of creation,
A pearl
In the ocean of humanity.

In the Still of Night

In the still of night
A candle prayed,
"O Lord,
Let me light the way in the dark of night,
That the weary and the traveler find their way,
And I, but a lowly candle,
Be a torch ashine, a shining light."

In the still of night
A candle prayed,
"O Lord,
May I forever be as I am,
Never weep even a drop of self away,
A candle whole, unscathed,
Never lit by night, neither lit by day."

God granted both candles their wish.
The first,
With joy and thankfulness,
Sacrificed itself to flame and light,
A guide for weary travelers,
Strangers afoot in the dark of night.

The second
Prideful, whole and cold,
Remained alone on a dark and dusty shelf,
Devoid of purpose, arrogant,
Ever filled with self.

We are as candles.
It is ours to choose,
To be illumined or not,
To gain or lose.

Innocent Flower

Innocent flower,
How peacefully you dwell,
Free of war and violence,
Anger and malice.
We have much to learn from you.

Lovely flower,
How gracefully you dance,
How softly you sway
In zephyrs of spring, the breeze of summer.
How steadfast, resilient you remain
In gusty winds and pouring rain.
We have much to learn from you.

Fragrant flower,
How sweet your petals,
How fragrant your perfume,
How selflessly you share them.
We have much to learn from you.

Content flower,
How free of avarice and envy you are,
How calm your countenance,
How pleasing your gratitude.
We have much to learn from you.

Innocent flower,
May you and yours forever shine,
Perfume our lives,

Unfold your petals of wisdom before us,
For you have much to teach,
And, alas,
We are slow to learn!

Life's Journey

Life's journey,
Where do you lead us
Or do we,
Indeed, lead the way?
I am told
You are but a short, rushing river
That some, mistakenly,
Think long,
And the ship we travel
Is of our own making,
Its sails sewn by our own hands,
Its winds of our own breath,
Its destination
Of our own choosing.

Stony paths,
Hard and narrow,
Seemingly unforgiving,
Undoubtedly,
We must walk,
Though far greater
The wide, brightly lit avenues
Of kindliness and benevolence
Stretching out before us,
Beckoning,
To guide our way!

On what streams,
Meandering or straight,

High or low,
Will we flow?
By what brooks
Will we stroll and linger?
On whose welcoming banks
Will we find rest?
By what towering falls
Will astonishment
Penetrate deep into our souls,
Transform heart and thought,
Birth us anew,
Never to be the same?

Hillsides,
Assuredly,
We will climb.
Bridges, no doubt,
We will cross.
But what of sharp and craggy rocks?
On these will we waver,
Lose faith,
Be brought to naught?

And what of forests green and dense?
Through these,
Will we find our way?
Will life's journey reveal valleys of love,
Meadows caressed
By gentle winds of affection,
Bowers of roses
Lined with mirth and repose?

In what gardens
Will we dwell to give praise,
Swoon away,
Captivated by the fragrant jasmine of joy?
Will sweet-scented honeysuckle
Waft through our days?
Will we marvel,
Take delight,
In the shining petals
Of dahlias and daisies,
The bright faces
Of orchids and camellias?

Will we ponder,
Awed and amazed,
The flight of the honeybee
And the flutter of the butterfly,
Songbirds eager to nest and coo,
The warbling of the nightingale
Entranced, intoxicated,
By the rose?
Will the song of the lark
Sweeten our souls?
Will the hover of the hummingbird
Give pause for reflection,
Contemplation?
From orchestrations
Composed and written upon the wind,
What wisdom, music of the soul,
Will we hear,
Play on lute and harp of the heart,
Conduct in the symphony hall of life?

And should we ascend
A high,
Towering mountaintop,
How hard will be the climb?
Will life's mysteries unfold before us,
Glance by glance, gaze by gaze?
From such a lofty peak
What might we learn,
Recite aloud,
Record on the pages
Of the book of our lives?

And,
If perchance,
We come to an ocean
Of enlightenment and truth,
Will we hesitate to enter
Its edifying, pure waters,
Or will we rush in with alacrity and joy,
Dive its depths
For coral and pearls of great price,
And then,
Fearless and unafraid,
Ride its illuminating, cresting waves
Of brotherly love,
Compassionate understanding?
And should we be overcome with fear
And hesitation,
Will we stand upon the shore
Only to be thrown down
Upon the sands of happiness lost
By the harsh and biting winds of superstition,

Blindly followed traditions
That corrupt the mind,
Strangle the soul?

Life's journey –
Such challenge and mystery it presents!
Its gifts are peace and contentment,
Wonderment and joy.
But should we stumble and fall,
Even lose our way
Along the paths we tread,
Still,
From these
We can arise,
Learn,
Find the path best chosen.

During the fleeting days and nights,
The winter cold and the summer heat,
The springtime zephyrs and howling winds
Of life's journey,
May we always remember,
Never forget,
Life is a gift given –
A gift too often neglected,
Taken for granted!

Like a Child

Like a child,
Pure of thought and intent,
Gleeful, joyous, happy at play,
Might this, too, we be?

Like a child,
Full of awe and wonder,
Hopes and dreams,
Might this, too, we be?

Like a child,
Eager to learn, willing to try,
Laughter unrestrained, unapologetic,
Might this, too, we be?

Like a child –
Heart pure,
Even as salubrious waters from summits on high;
Spirit joyous, lively, content,
Unafraid to love and be loved,
A soulful frolicking wind
Flowing across fields of bright tomorrows,
Windflowers of sunlit, fruitful years;
Nature innocent and gentle,
Imagination eager to stretch and dance;
Mind open,
Keen to explore, grasp and understand –
May we all,
Each and every one,

Arise,
Grow and mature day by day,
That peace and tranquility,
Love and justice,
Even as play,
Be the lot of every child.

Like the Passing of the Seasons

Beauty without,
Like the passing of the seasons,
Comes and goes,
Lasts for but awhile.
Beauty within,
Like an endless spring,
Blooms forever,
Its blossoms fragrant,
Its flowers sweet.

A life bereft
Of truth and understanding,
Like a barren tree,
Bears not the fruits of wisdom and joy.
True understanding,
Like the fragrance of the rose,
Attracts the nightingales of wisdom,
Causes them, in ecstasy, to circle about!

Keen sight
Serves the eagle well,
Without it, hunger would be its lot,
For it could never catch its prey!
If one be keen of vision, even possess an eagle eye
For worldly things and the world without,
Of what avail would this be,
If one be blind within,
And the soul, stumbling and lost
Could never find its way?

Love of self,
Like creatures that tunnel and crawl,
Moves on its belly, content and assured,
Drawn to the depths of darkness,
Its greatest fear exposure to light!
Love of humanity,
A fruited, flowering garden,
Comely and diverse,
Its skirt spread wide,
Its verdant avenues enlightened,
Rendezvouses with sunlight,
Bears succulent fruit,
Flowers fragrant and sweet,
Finds rest,
Abiding peace in moonlight,
Its nocturnal retreat!

One sight temporal,
The other eternal,
Far better that we have both!
For does not the sojourn of the soul,
Unlike the fragrance of the flower,
The succulence of fruit
Or the flight of the bird,
Transcend this earthly realm of dust,
This nether life?
For whispering winds ever proclaim
To the dove of the heart and eagle of the soul,
"Ethereal skies beckon you to realms beyond,
For yours is the inimitable gift
Of eternal flight!"

Little Daffodil

Little daffodil,
How you delight my heart!
In you I see
Queenly beauty crowned in gold,
Your humble,
Vernal throne of green
A testament to your humility.
In you I see
The gentle kiss of sunlight,
And from whispering winds
That woo and caress,
I hear the call of renewal,
The sounds of spring.

Gentle flower,
I have missed you so!
My longing eyes,
Too long accustomed
To winter's scenes of snowy white
And clouds of gray,
Give thanks
For your timely return,
Praise to the One
Who breathed deep into Nature's bosom
The breath of life,
Brilliant light and obsidian darkness,
The sound of silence and the music of sound,
Mystery to unfold,

Profundity to unravel.
All creation takes solace in this!

With each spring,
Quietly, serenely,
You testify to enduring faithfulness,
Thrill heart and soul, charm the spirit,
Even as the nightingale
Is thrilled by the rose,
And birdsong charms the hearts
Of enamored trysting lovers,
Those who coo as doves
Perched high
On branches of undying love,
True and professed devotion.
Would that humanity
Follow your example!

Truths eternal
Are yours to share,
Ours to grasp.
Through gusting winds of trial
You stand strong,
Never falter
Beneath Nature's showers,
Pouring rains that challenge,
Test your resolve.
From these you emerge
Poised and composed, unscathed,
Your golden visage
A testimony
To gratitude and hope,
The triumph of perseverance.

Sweet daffodil,
How you shine!
Your comely countenance
Is alluring,
A portrait of peace and contentment.
Your surrender,
Complete, unquestioned,
To the loving embrace of spring
Is unshakable, undeniable.
Such wisdom and understanding
You possess,
Such wonderment you excite!

Dearly loved flower,
Each year I await you,
The sweetness of your smile,
The timeless lessons you teach,
The gift of spring that you are!
In you I see a glimpse of Heaven,
A gleam of heavenly grace.

Beloved daffodil,
Unassuming,
Fashioned by Love
In the trellised gardens
Of His acceptance and pleasure,
In you are undeniable tokens
Of godliness and goodness,
Perfection and bounty,
Stories to ponder,
Poems to write.

Lovely daffodil,
Floral princess robed in gold,
I can write no more,
Though my soul is overflowing
With unwritten lines of the heart,
For these must wait for another time,
Another season,
When you emerge once again
In vernal splendor
To touch my heart,
Enrich my soul,
Delight my eyes,
Once more!

Little Fish in a Little Pond

Little fish
In a little pond,
How small your world,
Though you think it big,
How lonely your existence,
Though you think it full.

Divided humanity
On a tiny planet,
How small your world,
Though you think it big,
How fleeting earthly existence,
Though you think it long.

All peoples,
Young and old,
On our tiny planet,
Be as one,
Gentle waves and refreshing waters
Of one sea.
Be as fish, diverse, multicolored,
Swimming in one ocean,
Coexisting in peace.

But be not a little fish
In a little pond –
The division and separation
Of our own making!

Little Leaf

Little leaf
Stirred by the winds of time,
Winter gales and summer breezes,
Springtime zephyrs, the winds of fall,
Would that I could be as you are,
Blown by winds yet unyielding,
Holding firm, ever green,
To the branch.

Little leaf
Blowing in the wind,
I see you lively and content,
Steadfast and strong,
Never knowing loneliness or despair,
Ever observant
Of Mother Nature's commands.

Little leaf
Stirred by the winds of time,
In you I see wisdom and humility,
The path to joy,
Wonderment and meaning.
The lessons you teach
Deserve to be pondered,
Thoroughly grasped,
For though simple,
They are truly profound –
We need but eyes to see,
Depth within to understand.

Lonely Parrot in a Gilded Cage

Lonely parrot
In a gilded cage,
Alone, forlorn,
Your vibrant colors, exquisite beauty,
Fade in the darkness of captivity's gloom!
Creation weeps tears of sorrow,
Blowing winds lament,
Cry out for freedom, release,
On your behalf!

Your bright, playful nature,
Clever wit,
Where have they fled?
Your flight in skies of blue,
Sunlit gardens of avian delight,
Are now but fallen dreams,
Painful remembrance, pangs of longing!
Is this what I see in your eyes,
Hear from the siren silence of your voice?

Your plight of freedom lost,
Joys of life stolen and denied,
Grieve Mother Nature, weigh upon Her heart!
And how this must grieve you
And the faithful flocks circling round,
Unwilling you be forgotten!

Do children stop to greet you,
Wish you well, hope to see you fly?

Do passersby see you,
Ponder your being,
Show compassion for your plight,
Or is it but the gilded cage,
Shiny and bright, fancy and strong,
They see, appreciate and admire?
And if this be so,
How blind they must be!

Lonely parrot
In a gilded cage,
Do you see,
As do I,
Trees stretching, enamored of the sky,
Succulent, sweet fruit glistening in daylight sun,
Butterflies, free of care, regally attired,
Fluttering flower to flower,
Birds dancing blossom to blossom,
Flying branch to branch,
Soaring high and long,
Nesting in love,
Dwelling in peace?

Can you hear,
O bird of beauty,
The gentle laughter of clouds above,
The poignant cry of the wind
Addressing earth and heaven and all that is?
Can you hear it saying, breath by breath,
"I grieve at your plight,
The imprisonment you bear!
But stranger, still,
That the bird of the human heart,

The flight of the soul,
Can be imprisoned in a gilded cage
Fashioned from the false gold and gods
Of self and desire, of avarice and pride!"

In the deep silence that follows,
My soul,
Now stirred to ponder and reflect,
Asks of lessons learned,
Wisdom acquired
From this lonely parrot in a gilded cage
Held fast in the grip of confinement,
Flight and life, tree and sky denied.

With time
My soul responds –
A dwelling place of riches and gold
Gives neither meaning nor joy
To bird or man,
But, rather,
It is freedom to live and soar
The outspread immensity of life and purpose,
Fly the heavenly realms of gifts natural and acquired,
Ride the ever-flowing, salubrious winds of contentment,
Rise high in the beckoning skies of true liberty,
Happiness,
God-given rights!

Love Is the Begetter of All Good

Reality is the begetter of mystery.
Mystery is the begetter of reality.
Rapture is the begetter of wonderment.
Wonderment is the begetter of rapture.
Love is the begetter of all good.

Justice is the begetter of peace.
Peace is the begetter of justice.
Truth is the begetter of oneness.
Oneness is the begetter of truth.
Love is the begetter of all good.

Fellowship is the begetter of concord.
Concord is the begetter of fellowship.
Purity is the begetter of sanctity.
Sanctity is the begetter of purity.
Love is the begetter of all good.

Kindliness is the begetter of compassion.
Compassion is the begetter of kindliness.
Generosity is the begetter of charity.
Charity is the begetter of generosity.
Love is the begetter of all good.

Detachment is the begetter of true understanding.
True understanding is the begetter of detachment.
Faith is the begetter of certitude.
Certitude is the begetter of faith.
Love is the begetter of all good.

Self-effacement is the begetter of perfections.
Perfections are the begetter of self-effacement.
Contentment is the begetter of tranquility.
Tranquility is the begetter of contentment.
Love is the begetter of all good.

Reflection is the begetter of profundity.
Profundity is the begetter of reflection.
Insight is the begetter of wisdom.
Wisdom is the begetter of insight.
Love is the begetter of all good.

Encouragement is the begetter of perseverance.
Perseverance is the begetter of encouragement.
Patience is the begetter of repose.
Repose is the begetter of patience.
Love is the begetter of all good.

Godliness is the begetter of virtue.
Virtue is the begetter of godliness.
Trust is the begetter of loyalty.
Loyalty is the begetter of trust.
Love is the begetter of all good.

All good is begotten.
All good is reciprocal.
Love is the begetter of virtuous reciprocity.
Love is the begetter of all good.

Love Remains the Same

Years pass,
Distance grows –
Love remains the same.

Paths walked,
Avenues strolled,
Near or far, dark or lit –
Love remains the same.

Disparate lands tread
With their highs and lows,
Some flowered, some bare –
Love remains the same.

Life proffers what it will
From flowing streams of change,
But love,
Pure, true,
The grand elixir,
Like the Sun,
Ever remains the same.

Love, Heal Me!

I thought I heard the planet plaintively cry,
Love,
Heal me!
For I am yours and you are mine!
Heal me!

I thought I heard the ocean roar,
Love,
Heal me!
For I am yours and you are mine!
Heal me!

I thought I heard beseeching, blowing winds shout,
Love,
Heal me!
For I am yours and you are mine!
Heal me!

I thought I heard humanity, woeful, in pain, cry out,
Love,
Heal me!
For I am yours and you are mine!
Heal me!

I thought I heard my searching soul pray,
Love,
Heal me!
For I am yours and you are mine!
Heal me!

Quietly,
I waited for a response.
It was then I seemed to hear
The indwelling voice of the Beloved say,
"My love flows as a rushing river without end,
Surges as an endless sea –
But to what avail,
If you approach not my shores
And humanity, prideful,
Ride not my billowing,
Towering waves?"

I opened my eyes
To find love all around,
And, painfully,
Hardened hearts eager to deny it,
Unwilling to welcome it,
Let it in.

With love
Is the healing of all things,
Without it,
Only emptiness and pain!

Love, Unfold Me!

Love,
Unfold me
As spring unfolds blossom and bloom,
As the rose unfolds petal and perfume,
As the bird unfolds its wings,
As the nightingale unfolds melody and adoration.

Love,
Unfold me
As the sun unfolds its light.
As the night unfolds the stars,
As the moon unfolds moonglow.

Love,
Unfold me
As autumn unfolds red and gold,
As the tree unfolds the fruit,
As the land unfolds the grain.

Love,
Unfold me
As the songbird unfolds song,
As mourning doves unfold cooing from their nest,
As the wind unfolds the rustling of the leaves,
As the murmuring brook unfolds its quiet tales.

Love,
Unfold me
As generosity unfolds charity

As kindliness unfolds a smile,
As righteousness unfolds goodness,
As justice unfolds fairness, fair-mindedness.

Love,
Unfold me
As peace unfolds tranquility.
As an illumined heart unfolds joy.

Love,
Unfold me,
As the Beloved unfolds the lover,
For He calls to me
And my spirit longs for release,
And you, alone, sweet love,
Can unfold me,
Teach me the wonderment of love,
Give me life,
Set me free.

Lowly Though I Be

Upon whispering winds
Born of His shining Visage
I heard melodies of the spirit
That seemed to flow through me,
Call to me, awaken my soul,
Speak the hidden longings
Of my heart:

O my Beloved!
Lowly though I be,
Would that Thy beauteous glance
Fall upon me,
Illumine the dark and narrow corridors
Of my heart,
Bring to light the broad avenues
Of my soul.

Unworthy though I be,
Would that Thou wouldst walk with me,
Teach me Thy ways,
Lift me high that I might fly
The ethereal skies of Thy love,
Soar the heavens of Thy pleasure.

Though wanting of capacity,
Would that Thou wouldst unfold
By Thy hand and within my soul,
Ancient scrolls of truth;
Pour into the goblet of my heart

Thy ancient mystic Wine.
Then,
Inebriated and flushed with the heat of Thy love,
Rapture and ecstasy would consume me,
Enthrall my being,
Transform this floating speck of mortal dust
Into waves of spiritual light.

Though bereft of eloquence,
A clever pen and words to entice,
Would that Thou wouldst grant me
Ancient poems of the spirit to stir my soul,
Burn to ash illusion and fancy;
Bestow upon me
Rousing melodies of gleaming love
Intoned in splendor
And chanted by the maids of Heaven,
That my soul offer praise and thanksgiving
For all that Thou art,
Hast ever been,
Shalt ever be.

My heart now roused to a feverish pitch,
My soul aflame,
My being on fire,
Unable to constrain itself,
Cried out:

O my Beloved!
O Sanctuary of my soul!
Might such grace and bounty,
Gifts of spirit, mind and heart,
Be mine?

From hidden realms deep within,
Where the seat of His throne resides,
I seemed to hear Him say in the sweetest of tones,
Holy and melodious,
"O child of the God of love,
Be assured!
For I am yours
And you are Mine!
With heart pure and sincere
You sought Me,
Longed for My Presence,
The ecstasy of My love.
Though wayward,
You beseeched Me,
Yearned to walk the sacred path
Of love's command,
Heard My Call.

Such is the way of lovers,
And I,
The All-Loving,
The Well-Beloved,
Answer the call of all,
Who,
Pure of heart and untrammeled of mind,
Seek Me.
These I hear.
These I see.
These I lift to the exalted retreats of Paradise –
The spiritually glorious,
Ineffably fragrant,
Inimitable,
Rose garden of the heart."

Moonlight of Love

Descend,
O moonlight of love,
Illuminate the soul of humanity
With radiant, splendrous light,
For it calls to you,
Seeks illumination,
Your brilliant rays of love,
Onrushing waves of enlightenment,
That the darkness of humanity's night
Forever be dispelled.

Heavenly light of love,
Shine upon all peoples
As the moon shines upon jasmine and hyacinth,
Resting trees and sleepy mountain passes
In the still of night,
That humanity be illumined,
Souls radiate love,
Minds be enlightened,
Hearts shine bright with loving kindness,
Generosity and goodwill.
Only then
Will the lights of joy and happiness,
Cooperation and contentment,
Shine.

Moonlight of love,
Illuminate the path to peace,
To the trellised gardens of a united humanity,

Where the rose of love blooms
And nightingales of justice warble melodies
Of oneness and prosperity,
Where gentle winds of the spirit
Whisper songs and tales
Of dreams fulfilled,
Hearts at rest,
Children safe at play.

Glorious light of love,
Shine!
Illumine hearts and souls,
That all peoples surrender to your light
Even as the midnight moon
Surrenders to the light of the sun,
For only in this
Can humanity find its way,
Only in this
Will humanity not stumble and fall
To rise no more,
To forego
Its long-promised destiny.

My Soul Yearns to Fly

O,
How my soul yearns to fly
In skies beyond the blue,
To traverse the heavens, stars and space,
And sail the infinite
High upon winds of the spirit
And godly flows
Of resignation
And contentment.

O,
How I long to dance
Upon the mystic breeze
Of purity and understanding,
That my soul see truth,
Unhampered by whim
And daily care,
The dross
Of this nether world.

O,
How I dream of swimming
In oceans of meaning,
Rising high
With each heaving, thrusting wave,
And diving deep the seas of mystery,
Their warm, inviting waters
Gentle caresses of love
And wisdom.

O,
How I yearn
For all these things
Until,
Once again,
I fly the supernal skies of Revelation,
Swim the vast oceans of reality and truth,
And traverse,
With the Beloved as my guide,
All worldly attachment and illusion,
And rest in the sanctified abode
Of peace, wonderment,
Abiding love.

Mystic Fire

A flirtation with brevity and rhyme

Mystic fire
In my heart does rage,
Would that I could capture it
That it rush like a river,
Flow like a stream,
My hapless pen
Put it to the page!

Mystic love
In my soul does dance and dwell,
O that its enchanting stories
With the ink of the heart,
The fire of the soul,
My feeble pen could tell!

Mystic wine,
Heaven's sparkling ruby draught,
Intoxicates me so,
'Tis why from the wine cup
I dare not go!
Free of its madness,
My sanity would wane,
My spirit, distraught and bewildered,
Would be as naught,
Sobriety, my bosom bane!

Mystic fire,
Only this I ask,
That you burn away impurity and dross,
That the phoenix of love arise within,
Blazing and free,
And fly the mystic skies of the heart,
For therein lies the secret
Of love's boundless eternity!

Old Friend

A farewell to an old pine tree

Old friend,
Now gone,
You stood tall and green
In younger years,
When spring and showers
Smiled upon you,
And the Sun,
So pleased with your stretching boughs,
Nurtured you.

I recall well
Your youthful days,
Your jesting with bird and breeze,
Your steadfastness in storm and gale,
Your quiet beauty in days of snow.
Your natural charm and loveliness in moonlight.

Now gone
But not forgotten,
You live on in memory and soil,
Verdant visages, that, like you,
Tell tales of Nature's rhythms and rhymes,
Her love for diversity and beauty,
Her inviolable, unchanging decree
Proclaiming to all creation
The grand mystery,
Timelessness,
Of the cycle of life.

One Mighty Drop

One mighty drop,
Infinite in its power,
Relentless in its fall,
Fell upon the heart and watered the soul
Of a disillusioned mankind.

From this drop
Came seas of surging hope and love,
Billowing oceans of charity and generosity,
Gushing rivers of compassion and forgiveness,
Every virtue that ever was
Or ever will be.
Humanity's hard crust of dissension and hate
Began to dissolve.
Antiquated structures,
Their facade now washed away,
Were exposed,
Their promise swept away.
Outworn and effete institutions
Began to founder,
Then fail,
So powerful was that drop.

Humanity,
Imbued with a new and penetrating vision,
Witnessed flowing, salubrious streams
Of unforeseen possibilities,
All that might be.
Towering falls of understanding

Gave rise
To a new and wondrous grasp
Of spiritual realities,
And rushing rapids of knowledge
Flowed from pole to pole,
Heart to heart,
Transforming the world of thought
And innermost world of spirit.

Human conscience
Was awakened, enlightened.
Energies of interdependence and oneness
Were released
Reviving and refreshing the soul of mankind.
Flowing waters of equity and diversity
Descended from on high
Refreshing the still, reflective ponds
Of unfailing wisdom
And keen insight.

From this drop,
Some,
Inimical to its purity,
Drowned in its unyielding depths.
Others were swept away by its mighty force,
So dark were their hearts,
So grave their misdeeds.
Still others,
Heedless,
Unrepentant,
Will meet the same fate.

From this mighty drop –
The timeless, supernal,
Conquering sea of invincible Truth –
Evil and injustice will perish,
Hope and love, peace and joy will flourish,
Justice and universal prosperity
Will, at last,
Triumph,
Their standards,
Blown by victorious winds,
Raised high.

Time, alone,
Will reveal the unbounded potency
Of this mighty drop.
Newborn, revitalizing streams
Of humanity's movement towards unity,
Albeit one of trial and travail,
Testify to its enduring power.
The illumined heart and sanctified soul,
Transformed by its purifying character,
Proclaim its greatness,
Augur well
For its ancient,
Life-giving waters.

Only This I Ask of Thee!

O Beloved of my being!
Let me swoon away
And fly the zephyrs of the soul,
Then plunge the ocean depths of faith
Where pearls of spiritual insights glow,
And then, immersed in rapturous prayer,
May I die to all except Thy holy Word,
This, not more, is all I ask,
All I ask of Thee!

O Possessor of my soul!
Let me be as naught,
Not even a spider upon the wall
Or an ant upon a mound,
But free of self, in search of Thee,
In this, Thy Promised Day,
Only this, not more, I wish to be,
Only this I ask of Thee!

O Quickener of souls,
Bearer of heavenly delights!
Let my heart be firm of faith,
A fiery torch of kindly light,
A lamp of burning love,
A flame pure and bright!
Of this I ask,
Though the path be hard,
The journey never-ending –
But what care of this have I,

For I know the destination,
And, O how joyous,
How glorious the task!

Pain I Have Not

Pain I have not,
Only the pain in my heart.

Sorrow and grief I have not,
Only the sorrow and grief in my soul.

Burdens I have not,
Only the burdens that trouble the mind.

Pain, grief and burdens
I have not,
Only the knowledge of those brought low,
The sorrowful and the downcast,
Or when I behold the plight
Of the suffering and the oppressed.

Pain, grief and burdens
I have not,
Only when I see hopelessness
And despair,
The wrongfully accused,
Those denied justice,
Powerless to right the wrongs they suffer,
The horrors of war,
Stolen childhoods.

When love and compassion
Shine resplendent
And cruelty and injustice

No longer veil the light,
When they are a thing forgotten,
Relegated to the past,
Neither pain nor sorrow nor grief will I have,
No burden will I bear.

Paradise

Paradise,
I know you well.
I have held you in my hand,
Gazed upon you with adoring eyes,
Held you close,
O so close,
To soul and bosom,
There to awaken, vitalize my lowly heart,
Spread your vernal skirt wide as blowing winds
Moved by the rhythms of spring,
Unfold like hyacinth and rose to please Sun and sky,
Adorn spiritual gardens of serenity and peace
Perfumed in sweet repose.

Heavenly script upon the page,
Begetter of luminous love and soaring joy,
Kindliness and contentment,
Your splendrous visage,
Intoxicating beauty and mystery,
Swelling,
Surging seas of profundity and rapture,
I cannot,
Nor will I ever,
Deny.

Paradise,
Salubrious flame of the Supernal,
Breathtaking,
Awe-inspiring is your power to set aflame

Heart and soul,
Beget,
Give wing to the phoenix of love,
That enkindled, aglow,
It traverse sacred realms within,
Realms to humble,
Dwarf Earth's loftiest skies,
Wondrous, alluring, though they be.

Your essence,
Inimitable holy reality,
Defies description.
Scholars and savants, saints and poets,
Though they try,
Are powerless to describe you,
Depict your beauty,
Portray your majesty,
Unravel your holy reality,
Sanctified transcendence.
You alone have such power.
Effulgent script of the Pen of Glory,
May you ever rest in hand,
Abide in heart,
Thrill and capture mind and soul,
For without you my soul would know
No rising dawn,
No brilliant, sunlit days,
Mystical, moonlit nights.

Paradise,
Across the distant reaches of time
And untold expanse of timelessness,
I am yours!

For this alone,
O beloved of my heart and mover of my soul,
Do I pray –
That as I walk the eternal path of the spirit,
Cross its hills and vales
And dwell in its gardens,
And assuredly as I am yours,
O life of my soul,
Please be mine!

Pilgrim in the Valley of Love

O my Beloved!
Thou seest this pilgrim in the valley of love
Distraught in his separation from Thee.

Thou seest this feeble soul,
His heart on fire in search of Thee,
His spirit yearning for Thee,
Even as a crying wind
Yearns to traverse forests green,
Distant lands and surging seas.

Thou seest,
O my Desired one!
This pilgrim wandering
The meads of adoration and valleys of longing
Wishing to praise Thee,
But to what avail,
For,
At the thought of praising Thee,
My tongue is mute,
My hand trembles, unable to move,
My fingers, bereft of strength,
Are unable to write.
My pen,
Aware of my plight,
Refuses the page,
My inkwell,
Now like desert sands,
Is dry.

Still,
O my Best -Beloved,
Unabashed, unashamed,
I seek to praise Thee,
Draw nigh,
Be acceptable
At Thy threshold.

Thou seest, O my Lord,
This pilgrim in the valley
Or rapturous love and longing
With empty hands,
Unworthy heart and soul,
Beseeching at the door of Thy mercy
To overlook my faults,
Forgive my sins which are as endless oceans
And boundless seas.

Or,
If it please Thee,
Leave me to wander the arid lands
Of separation from Thee,
For Thy pleasure is my pleasure,
Thy wish, my wish,
Thy command,
Whatever it may be,
My greatest joy and endless bounty
To obey,
And this,
In praise of Thee!

Pillars of Humanity

Pillars of humanity,
How you tremble so!
It seems your collapse,
Stone by stone, day by day,
Is drawing nigh,
A mere inevitability!
Could it be
The weight of tyranny and injustice,
Self-interest and greed,
Has, at last,
Brought you low,
Soon to be no more than
Strewn rubble on forgotten ground!
The rumblings of our times,
Shaking you to your very core,
Testify to your hard, fated fall,
Your ruinous end,
As do keen, discerning eyes!

Your pillars,
Once straight and strong,
Now quake land to land, pole to pole,
Leaving neither heart nor town, soul nor city,
Unshaken by the mighty tremors of a New Day,
A Day in which the pillars of humanity
Will be, must be!
Raised anew on solid ground,
The very bedrock of justice and unity!

Pillars of humanity,
Your impending fall,
The crumbling of your columns,
Is plain to see,
For your stones of justice are weak,
Your support of injustice strong.
How strange, how very strange!
Your once-grand pillars,
Raised to hold aloft peace and harmony,
Raise high the rights of all peoples,
Equity for all,
Totter before us,
Soon to be no more,
Stone forgotten,
Forgotten quite!

But mighty pillars strong and new,
Unfailing in their support of justice,
Will, without fail,
Be raised in your stead
To stand long and strong,
Even as the mighty,
Ancient pillars of the heavens
Uphold the sun by day
The moon and stars by night.
Illumined by the light of truth,
They will be raised high for all mankind to see
And will, in the fullness of time,
Support the shining dome
Of peace and prosperity for all peoples,
The advancement and well-being
Of all mankind.
They will reach beyond the heavens

To hold high a world-embracing civilization
Shining in the light of a New Day,
A Day of righteousness and justice for all,
Of unity and diversity,
Of the advancement of every human endeavour.

Tottering pillars of humanity,
Be assured of this –
It is we,
A spiritually rejuvenated, united humanity
Empowered by the glorious energies of the New Day
Who will raise them high and raise them strong,
We who will make firm their foundation,
We who will accomplish the task,
Day by day and hour by hour,
One radiant heart,
One righteous deed,
One noble act,
One clarion call,
At a time!

Poppy Fields of Red and Gold

*In remembrance and honor of the God-intoxicated lovers who
have given their lives for the love of Truth, the betterment of all
mankind, justice and prosperity of all peoples*

Poppy fields
Of red and gold,
Blooming ballerinas of wondrous beauty,
Gracefully, magically,
You move and dance to rhythms
Played on springtime zephyrs,
Unfolding summer winds!
But is it the wind
That thrills and stirs you so,
Or some mystical, unseen, force
At the heart of creation
And the expanse of the heavens
That calls to you
As the morn calls to light
And dusk calls to night?

Poppy fields,
Is it the warbling of songbirds
Wafting from near and far
That beckons,
Gives rise to your skyward gaze,
Waving fields of red and gold?
Or is it the mournful cry of easterly winds
Reciting, verse and line,
The martyr's tale?

And if it be
The tale of the martyrs,
Those noble,
Intoxicated lovers
Inebriated by the ruby wine
Of the Loved One's beauty
From the chalice of His Presence,
Then let us hear each word,
Fraught, crimson red,
And every line,
Telling, brilliant gold,
With moving,
Heart-wrenching clarity.
This you can do,
For your luminous petals,
Submissive to sun and glory,
Betoken sacrifice and nobility.

Poppy fields
Crimson red and brilliant gold,
Speak aloud! Have no fear!
The Lord, God, will protect you!
Let the seeker and the righteous,
The weary and the oppressed,
Find enlightenment, awe and wonder,
In the martyr's love and devotion,
Bravery and consecration of soul,
That their hearts, too,
Become a torch afire,
Their coursing crimson blood
A river of raging love.

How truly
The flame of the Loved One's beauty

Does warm and brighten
The outstretched heavens
Of the lover's heart,
Illuminate,
Bathe in light
The furthermost depths of the soul
To reveal a Truth so wondrous,
A Reality so grand,
As to pale creation,
Cause it,
But a humble vassal,
Awestruck,
To bow down in consternation,
Surrender its all
As nothing,
Nothing quite!

And such a tale it is!
God-intoxicated lovers
Persecuted, laid low,
Violated by the vile sword of hate
And cruel, wanton blade
Of the ravenous and the treacherous,
The ungodly and willfully blind,
Those who,
In the guise of humans
Are but ravenous wolves
That devour the body but never the soul,
Steal the breath of the faithful
But never the breath of faith,
Condemn to death the human heart
But never its pure, pulsating love!
O how pitiful!
Born human,

They prefer to roam with delight
The dark, damp forests
Of damned illusion,
Benighted self-love,
Covetousness and greed.

O how poignant,
Magnificent,
The martyr's tale!
Those holy souls,
Ever ablaze with the love of God,
Now soar,
Flaming phoenixes of love and certitude,
In skies of glory,
Ride winds of truth and circle round
As the nightingale circles the rose,
The Mystic Garden of His Presence,
The fragrant Rose of His love.

Poppy fields
Of red and gold,
Be not shy!
Cry aloud the martyr's tale!
Teach us the martyr's song
That we may intone its melody,
Find inebriation in each and every note,
Then arise and soar,
Faithful, unafraid,
Phoenix-like,
In heavenly realms
Only God-intoxicated lovers
Know,
Are wont to fly.

Power of Truth

Power of truth,
Mount your steed,
Indomitable stallion of galloping light,
Then shine forth,
Sword of effulgent truth in hand,
To illuminate darkness,
Dispel falsehood,
Banish the false,
Expose the falsehearted!

Ride into battle,
Sword raised high,
Blade blazing, triumphant,
That all might see your mighty blows,
Powerful, transforming hand!

Knight in armament of shining light,
Rush forth,
Spare not lie nor slander,
Language to confound, discomfit,
Pillage or plunder.
Flash your sword of timeless radiance
That truth prevail,
Falsity perish to be no more!

Power of truth,
Show no mercy!
Ride hard and long!
Bring to your aid your all-conquering legions

Of godliness and goodness,
That victory be swift and assured
And lying tales, violation and injustice
Be vanquished, trampled under,
Their dust ignominiously buried
In the desolate tomb of oblivion,
Never to rise again!

Rhythms of Love

Rhythms of love
Flow as meandering streams
Through space and time,
The placeless and eternity,
Whispering winds,
Quantum mysteries,
Subtle realities;
Rhythms
That give rise to waves of light,
The flight of birds,
Rustling leaves,
The throbbing lover's heart.

Rhythms of love
Span the ages,
Cause the seasons to dance
In pulsations of pink and white,
Violet and blue, red and gold,
Every color that is,
Every hue
That God ever painted;
Rhythms
That give birth to blossom and bloom,
Vine and fruit, the growing branch,
Blowing winds of winter,
The quiet nights of summer.

Rhythms of love
Drive the surging seas,

Raise high their billowing waves,
Cause longing waters
To rush to awaiting, patient shores;
Rhythms
That move hearts to care,
Souls to love,
Lovers to tryst, marry,
Be as one.

Rhythms of love
Flow through truth and creation,
The seen and unseen,
All peoples, all things,
Except the cold and lifeless heart,
It, alone, is impervious
To their life-giving pulsations,
Unwilling to dance
To their timeless, unifying rhythms!

Search in the Dust

Search in the dust,
Explore dessert sands if you must,
But to what avail
If the sea of wisdom and knowledge,
The billowing ocean of truth you seek?

Traverse hill and vale,
Wander land to land,
A vagabond without care or dream,
But if the heavens of mystic wonderment
Be your calling,
Leave behind all worldly thought,
Earthly desire,
For these,
To the bird of the spirit,
Are naught but broken branches,
Deceiving mire.

Then,
Zealous,
Unafraid,
A mighty eagle of affection and longing,
Spread wide your spiritual wings,
Sail the godly breeze,
Glide ethereal winds,
Conquer cloud and sky,
And then,
In the lofty heavens of the heart,

Fly! mighty eagle!
Fly!

If the rose of love
Be your goal,
Leave behind the raven's song,
The cawing of the crow,
Then warble sweet melodies of the heart,
Even as a nightingale perfumed in adoration,
A songbird swooning away
In the rose garden
Of love's rapturous intoxication.

If the ocean of truth you seek,
If the heavens of wonderment
Be your heart's desire,
If the rose of love be your hope,
Then purge the heart and cleanse the soul,
For the ocean of truth,
The heavens of wonderment,
The rose of love,
Are all within
If one but see and hear,
Listen and turn to,
The Beloved,
He for Whom
Oceans billow and seas surge,
He for Whom
Sun and Moon, and heavens shine,
He for Whom
The rose of love grows and unfolds
To adorn and perfume
The beauteous garden
Of the lover's heart.

Shadows of Imagination

Shadows of imagination,
Illusory, vile,
Transitory darkness
Cowering before Sun and dawn,
Fleeting arrogance and pride dispelled by light,
You are as nothing!
For what, then, do you linger?

The Sun has risen!
Feel its warming rays,
The effulgent power of its light!
Assuredly,
Dread has overcome you!
Your condign demise is undeniable,
Final,
Irreversible,
Long overdue!

Shadows of oppression and tyranny,
Deceit and transgression,
You are naught
But the bleak, cold darkness
Of destruction and misery,
The black night of pain and strife
Assailing the soul of humanity.
Soon your days will be ended,
Your ungodly remains consigned
To the crypt of oblivion

Beneath the tombstone
Of the disgraced.

And yet,
Fools that you are,
You persist,
Abhorred and unwanted
Except by the corrupt,
The tyrant and the unjust!
These are they,
Bereft of generosity and goodwill,
Altruism and compassion,
For whom truthfulness is but a plaything,
Trustworthiness but a toy!

Shadows of evil,
How wretched your shame,
Your servile ignominy!
How infamous your lack of remorse!
You are but fleeting arrows
Flung from baneful bows
Of the heartless, the uncaring!
These hurl their poison darts
At the innocent,
Those that dare defy them!

Shadows of delusion and hurt,
You are as the passing of night just before dawn!
Soon will the evil,
Baneful hands that employ you
Be chained up,
Brought down,
Unable to win or triumph!

Soon,
Even as a speck of dust that never was,
Their hands of blight and woe
Will be but a fleeting fancy
Consigned to the mire.
Assuredly,
With the rising of the Sun,
The lights of justice and truth will triumph,
Conquer all,
Dispel every lingering, evil shadow
That ever was!

Your demise
Will be as the blinking of an eye!
Unrepentant,
Lame and abandoned,
Imprisoned in the dark, damp caverns
Of your shameful, nether life,
You will pass with none to mourn you
Or call you to mind!

With the coming of dawn
And the rising Sun,
The light of love and affection will shine!
Glorious rays of spirituality will flood Earth and heart,
Give rise to the limitless,
Lustrous beauty of oneness,
The gleaming charm and allure of diversity!
Heartwarming beams of happiness and joy,
Tranquility and contentment,
Will shine upon all peoples,
And the glorious effulgence
Of peace and harmony

Will transform the very soul
Of all mankind!

Such is the power
Of the rising Sun of wisdom and truth!
Such are its life-giving rays!
Such is the splendor of the dawn
Of the New Day,
The luminous, brilliant destiny
Of all peoples,
All humanity!

Shell Without a Pearl

Heart cold and damp,
Dark and dim,
Dwelling place of shadows, abhorrent of the light –
Shell without a pearl!

Soul self-enamored,
Selfish, self-absorbed,
Blind to one's shortcomings –
Shell without a pearl!

Heart without charity,
Devoid of generosity,
Compassion but a vague phantasm –
Shell without a pearl!

Soul of shadows,
Black cave of spiritual night,
Home to bats of darkness –
Shell without a pearl!

Heart feigning friendship,
Goodness and cheer,
Inclined to connive and deceive –
Shell without a pearl!

Heart without love,
Kindliness and care,
Sincerity and understanding –
Soul without a spirit,

Spirit without a life,
Life without meaning,
Shell without a pearl!

Shine for Me!

Sun,
Brilliant orb,
Shine for me!
Illumine my soul,
For I am a lover of the light
And seek the effulgent Orb
Of His Presence!

Moon,
Luminous mirror,
Glow for me!
Illuminate my inner being,
Enlighten my spirit,
For you are the splendrous light of night,
My heavenly guide,
And my soul has lost its way!

Night,
Ethereal palette of ebony and light,
Romance the stars for me,
That they unfold each scintillating mystery,
Each ancient beam of mystic truth,
And I, captive to their light,
Am illumined and refreshed
In the resplendent ecstasy
Of heavenly wonder!

Rose,
Flower sublime,

Perfume heart and soul,
The breeze of day and the still of night!
Do this for me,
That my heart unfold in fragrant purity
And my soul,
Alive to your godly essence,
Waft sweet savours of spiritual redolence,
Even as an April breeze wafting vernal tidings
Of all things made new,
That this be a sign of hope for me!

Wind,
Nature's keeper
Of tales of old and stories new,
Whisper tales of love for me
That resound beyond the heavens,
Reach beyond the stars,
That my heart may hear, in peals of joy,
The lovers' tales you tell,
And my soul dance
To mystic, edifying love!

Songbirds,
Angelic marvels
Of melody and flight,
Trill and warble your songs for me,
For I long to hear
The melodies of the spheres,
Celestial harmonies
From the pen of saints and angels
Played on harp and lute
To the eternal accompaniment
Of faithfulness.

Nature,
Beloved mother of all we see,
Of beauty and reciprocity,
Unveil your hidden mysteries,
All that you know!
Unfold your truths before me!
Open the book of your wonders,
For my heart, forlorn,
And my soul, heavy and dark,
Cry out to you,
And you,
Mother of mystery,
Possess the elixir of mystic knowledge
That, alone,
Can relieve my pangs of sorrow,
The weeping of my soul,
My tearful, crying eyes!

Beloved mother,
Have pity on this supplicant!
Water the barren lands of my soul
With rushing rivers of righteousness,
Salubrious streams proclaiming the sublime,
Reflection pools and ponds with truths to ponder,
That I may strive anew, seek the luminous path
To the All-Glorious Beloved
And attain,
Should it be His pleasure,
His Presence
In the hallowed precincts
Of His grace.
Then,
Revived,

Spiritually alive and renewed
By His holy,
Uplifting breaths of love,
I will wing my flight
And venture on,
Fearless and unafraid,
Victorious on the battlefields of love and truth
By the invincible sword of His Word
Wielded by the commanding power of His inspiration
For the salvation, resurrection and glory
Of all mankind.

Silent Snow and Quiet Winds

A brief reflection on the beauty of falling winter snow

Silent snow
And quiet winds
Paint sky and ground
In gleaming wonder,
Glimmering white.

Moonlight,
Nature's midnight sun,
Illumines each snowflake,
Whispers in flowing waves of splendor
Verse to accompany their graceful fall,
Intones brilliant melodies
To captivate the heart,
Enchant the soul,
Excite awe and wonder.

Silent snow
And quiet winds,
Winter's grand ballet
Performed on the ethereal,
Outspread stage
Of Nature's beauty and charm,
Dance through winter nights,
Enthrall our senses,
Awaken reflection on Nature's gifts,
Small and grand,

The mysteries and stories
She so skillfully tells.

Silent snow
And quiet winds,
We eagerly await you,
The beauteous ballet you dance,
The wondrous stories
You tell,
The magic of falling snow
On a moonlit winter's night!

Some Day I Will Fly

Some day I will fly,
When leaves yellow and wither
And winds of time,
Blowing hard,
Set them free from branch and twig,
Scatter them to stone and ground.

Some day I will fly,
When roots,
Once strong and deep,
Life giving,
Fail,
Find eternal rest
In the warm bosom
Of the earth
That held them close,
Gave them nurture.

Some day I will fly,
When bough and branch are bare,
Worldly blossoms bloom no more
And the sweet fruit of temporal existence
Is but a faded blossom
On the tree of evanescence.

Some day I will fly,
When winds blow and gales roar,
When the dust that I am blows away
And heart,

Tired at last,
Takes its rest
And crimson rivers of life,
Once quickly coursing,
Flow no more.

Some day I will fly
Lofty realms of the spirit
Beyond earth and sky,
Worldly cares and ephemeral pursuits,
Realms destined to call,
Bid me home.

Some day I will fly.
Till then
I will soar the ethereal realms within
And the heavens of kindly love without,
Soar the blue majestic skies
Of a purposeful, earthly life
Free of the dark clouds and pouring rains
That deny the oneness and rich beauty
Of human diversity,
And the peace and justice
Assuredly to be achieved
And flourish across the centuries
By the magnificent creation
We call humanity.

Songbird of Light and Love

Songbird of light and love,
Mystic warbler
From supernal realms divine,
Hear our cry!
The cry of babe and child,
The helpless and the hopeful,
The forlorn and ravaged of war,
The cry of the faithless and the faithful,
Peoples near and peoples far!

Soar high above cloud and wind,
Misery and despair,
Then dive,
Even as a holy falcon of glorious, transforming love
Into the pained, suffering soul of humanity!
Fly its skies!
Illuminate its heavens!
Then warble in tones of light and love,
Dazzling bliss and wonderment,
Your sweet, captivating melodies of the spirit!
Trill your timeless wisdom,
Your unchallengeable, ancient promise,
Your resounding songs of joy and happiness
In tones and melodies celeste!

Songbird of light and love,
Time is short
And the dark night of our times
Heavy to bear!

Banish the gloom of hate and contention,
Prejudice and greed,
With each illuminating flap of your wings,
With each energizing, holy breath!
Then warble as only you can
And as never before,
Your wondrous, unifying melodies
That all peoples be as one,
Alive to love,
Goodness and generosity,
The well-being of all,
Every godly gift!

Songbird of light and love,
Shine forth!
Sound your call
That our hearts respond with,
Yea, verily!
O songbird!
Yea, verily!
And then,
Soar and dive forevermore
The newly awakened chambers of our hearts
Accompanied by warbling hymns of hope,
Oneness and cooperation,
That ride upon your beams of spiritual light
And pulsating love
In the endless skies of the soul of humanity,
For nothing else,
O sweet songbird of the divine,
Can save us,
Teach us love and peace,
The wonderment
Of your song!

Songbirds, Sing for Me!

Songbirds,
Sing for me!
Warble melodies of springtime love
And soft summer night trysts
To warm the heart,
Revive the soul.

Trill,
As only you can,
Songs of endearing love
And timeless tales
Of lovers old and lovers new,
Vows of lovers faithful,
Love pure,
Lovers true.

Songbirds,
Sing for me!
Rejoice my soul!
Assure my heart,
That love and goodness,
Like sky and cloud
And forests of green
Will endure and abound,
That babes,
Like chicks nestled
In a lofty mountain nest,
Still sleep peacefully
At their mothers' breasts,

And children,
Filled with joy and glee,
Are safe at play.

Sing sweet melodies
Of assurance,
That truth and tenderness
Will always prevail,
That kindliness and affection,
Like fields of wind flowers,
Will forever
Spread wide their skirt.

Warble songs
Of people caring deeply
One for the other,
Of heavenly virtues ceaselessly proclaimed
From rushing rivers of the heart
To quiet streams of the soul,
From the flowered bowers of birth
To the high mountaintops
Of age and wisdom.

And,
If this you can do,
My soul will be at rest
And my heart find repose,
For the cries of the oppressed,
The neglected and the forgotten,
Blow hard upon the wind,
Leaving little else
To be heard.

Songbirds,
Sing for me!
Let me hear your sweet song,
Your warbles and your trills!
That hope and faith be renewed,
And melodies of love,
With the passage of time
And from the secure nest of oneness
Perched high
On the promised branch of justice
Be heard,
Intoned heart to heart
And warbled eternally
From the songbirds of the souls
Of all mankind.

Stories Nature Tells

Stories Nature tells
Are as vast as the heavens,
As telling as billowing seas,
As profound as ocean depths,
As moving as a meandering, springtime breeze.
These she softly whispers to the heart.
The soul, in hearing these,
Rejoices in their telling.

Melodies Nature plays
Are songs of love to sing,
Shout aloud,
Melodies that wind and sea and moonlight,
Enraptured lovers of their beauty,
Hear,
Clutch to breast,
Dance to
In pulsating waves and rhythms of joy.

Truths Nature lays bare, unfolds,
Are truths to free the soul,
Enlighten the mind,
Give wing to the bird of the spirit.
These flow profusely from Her pen
As sunlight radiates from the Sun,
Are as numbered as the leaves
Rustling awe and wonder in the grand forests of time.
With the break of day they begin to unfold,

With the fall of night they are laid bare
To ponder, challenge.

Nature has mysteries to unravel,
Wisdom, essence, to reveal.
In Her bosom
Hidden gems await discovery,
Profound insight to reveal their lustre,
Awaken them to the light,
Cause them to gleam forth
In brilliant rays of gemlike understanding.

Nature has stories to tell,
Tales of love and peace,
Glorious unity and wonderment
To be whispered heart to heart,
Soul to soul,
Shared in melodies of the spirit.
Ours is to listen,
Hear,
Take to heart,
Put to practice,
Her wondrous tales of profound love
For all that lives,
All that moves,
All that is.
In this,
She knows,
Alone,
Is humanity's salvation.

Stunned

Inspired by the Writings of Bahá'u'lláh

Stunned,
I marveled at His words
As they rose in holiness from the page,
Each word a brilliant sun rising from the dawn,
A shining orb at the height of day,
Mystery courting the black of night.

Each letter,
Joined in holy rapture
Word by word and upon the page,
Shone brightly, boldly,
A testimony to the Godhead, Vicegerency,
Each line quaking shibboleths old,
Trembling ways of yore.
Worlds seen and unseen
Stirred at their union,
Blazed forth in fiery love at their command.
Eternity,
Dwarfed, humbled, awestruck,
Took notice,
Bowed low.
Time and space,
Heedful,
Unfolded at their pleasure.

From the movement of each line,
East to eternity,

Came forth the spinning of the earth,
Awe and wonder
Spinning at the speed of astonishment.
Circling round each line,
As Saturn,
Adorned in rings of glory,
Circles the sun,
Were worlds, vast and holy,
Home to adoring angels,
Legions of seers and saints.
From each line was born the breeze of day
And winds of night,
Soaring eagles of truth
With wings of indomitable strength and power
To command the skies of justice and equity.

From each dotted "i"
I beheld a strong pillar
Of prophetic, revelatory light,
A torch lighted by the hand of God
Illuminating the pathway to the Beloved,
The sign of the upright and the noble,
The shining candle of the heart.

From each "t"
I beheld forests of green,
Mighty trees tall, verdant, stretching beyond infinity,
Their enthralled, enchanting leaves
Rustling mystic songs of love,
Hymns of praise,
Each leaf beseeching grace and bounty,
Prosperity and peace
For all mankind.

From each "o"
I beheld seas of sparkling,
Joyful drops of inspiration and revelation
Atop towering, billowing waves
Of meaning, purpose, infallibility,
Waves moved by dauntless, faithful winds,
Even as the ocean, dauntless, faithful,
Rushes to land and shore.

From every letter, word and line,
The turning of the page,
I beheld the Beloved's ethereal, wondrous script
Written on the horizon of the soul of humanity,
A script powering the visible and the invisible,
Birthing magnanimity, faith and love,
Giving wing to wisdom and volition,
Transforming seekers
Answering the call of the New Day.
These rushed forth
To the hallowed Sanctuary of His Presence
In the illumined garden of the heart,
For therein Manifest Love abides,
Waits patiently,
Bestows grace.

From His Word
I beheld wonders to rejoice the soul
And heal the sick,
Raise the downtrodden and enrich the poor,
Wonders to revive an ailing world,
Transform hate into love,
War into peace,
Separation into oneness,

Sorrow into joy –
Wonders sorely needed by a world in travail,
Wonders long sought by all peoples,
All mankind.

Sweet Perfume of Love

Sweet perfume of love,
Mystic elixir from the Hand of God,
Set free your redolence
That it penetrate my being,
Waft through my soul!
Descend in waves of fragrant love
From lofty retreats on high!
Come down,
In onrushing showers
Of incomparable, vitalizing fragrance!
Flow through me,
As a salubrious wind flows through
The petals of the rose,
Romances, teases with delight,
Jasmine and honeysuckle!
Free your ethereal bouquet,
Your sublime essence,
To enrapture, create me anew
From your heavenly,
Wafting savours!

Blow through the bowers of my being,
A zephyr of holiness from on high,
And perfume
The sadly languishing flowers within,
That they blossom and bloom
In brightly colored benevolence,
Unfold in splendrous,
Breathtaking beauty.

In the garden of my heart,
Lavishly splash your heavenly,
Pure fragrance of love,
That hyacinths of hope emerge and thrive,
And songbirds of joy,
Newly awakened to the sunrise of the spirit,
Warble songs of sweet delight,
Melodies to rejoice the hopeful heart.

Sweet perfume of love,
Be not shy!
Drench the dry and barren lands,
The withered hilltops,
The seeking, towering peaks
Of the reality within
With your heaven-scented,
Life-giving rains,
Your springtime showers
Of the soul!

Like a ravishing lover,
Envelop me!
Possess me!
Take me to your bosom,
Caring and warm!
Perfume the restless rivers
And surrendering streams
Of my heart!
Make redolent and calm
The restless,
Billowing waters of my soul,
That pearls of praise
And coral of contentment
Be discovered!

Penetrate the depths of my being!
Pour therein all the love
My soul can hold!
Then fill the passes and the ravines,
The yearning canyons
And the longing gorges
Of my being
With your sacred,
Godly scent!

Sweet perfume of love,
Upon the scroll of my heart
Write with the ink of mystic redolence
Poem and rhyme and mystery,
Verse to stretch across the ages,
Confirm seer and sage,
Guide the way,
Fill me with wonder
And astonishment!
I will ponder each line,
Hold it to my breast
As a mother holds her newborn child,
Recite it aloud for all to hear,
Inhale deeply
The sacred fragrance
You are!

Perfumed ballerina of love!
Dance!
Dance across my days and nights,
My aspirations and my dreams!
Dance to the melodies
Of your matchless floral notes!

Come to me
That I hold you close!
Then, as one,
We will dance to fragrant harmonies
Of undying, selfless love!

Sweet perfume of love,
Unfaltering ballerina sublime,
Perform fragrant fouettés,
Elegant, inspired,
Hyacinth-sweet grand jetés
To delight, amaze!
Together, inseparable,
Let us perform grand adagios of love
On the perfumed stage
Of eternity!

Perfume of love,
Perfume me!
Lavishly splash
Your fragrance upon me!
Then,
Perfumed in love,
I will be, at last,
Fully alive,
Redolent of soul,
Truly human!

Symphonies of Spring

Symphonies of spring
In the grand concert halls
Of life and love, beauty and art,
Play melodies upon soaring winds
And enraptured souls;
Dance rhapsodically upon moonbeams
That tease the dark of night
And radiate reveries that delight and inspire
Enlightened chambers of the heart;
Symphonies so beauteous and grand
That they resound deep within
And entice moonlight
To thrill love and lovers,
The spiritually illumined,
Those kind of heart.

Symphonies of spring
Warm brilliant rays
Of joyous springtime light.
These search out
Every flower, bloom, twig and petal,
That a note be played from each
In the major key of spring
And to the accompaniment of harmonies,
Vernal and lush,
That evoke ancient, ancestral song
Composed from the unfaltering pens
Of earth and sky

And transcribed on the sunlit pages
Of season and time.

Choruses of rustling leaves
Perform,
Unrehearsed, perfectly played,
Lyrical notes for all to hear.
Unwilling to be silenced,
Demanding to be heard,
They play on,
Encouraged
By flirtatious springtime breezes
Romancing color and bloom
Dawn till dusk,
Midnight, and the wee hours –
It is then they roam and dance,
Awaken sleeping flowers,
Bid them arise,
Beckon them to play.

Songbirds,
Grand masters of the concert hall,
Give rousing performances second to none,
Perform compositions to announce the dawn,
Pay tribute to love and beauty.
In the theatre of the rose,
Grand hall adorned and perfumed by its many petals,
Rose-intoxicated nightingales,
Yearning, unyielding lovers,
Swoon away,
Warble transporting songs of redolent love.

Perched on the branch of peace and tranquility,
Cooing doves,
Maestros in their own right,
Unfold mysteries of fidelity and devotion,
Lay bear the secret of enduring oneness.
Meadowlarks and blue jays,
Robins and cardinals,
These, too,
Take the stage,
Perform brilliantly,
Delight heart and ear,
Murmuring brooks
And cool mountain streams,
Quantum fields
Moving through field and flower,
All that is.

Butterflies,
Regally attired, never vain,
And eager to contribute their share,
Flutter about romancing springtime blooms,
Their mystical,
Vibrant,
But often subdued orchestrations
Masterfully played from fluttering wings
That God alone conceived and crafted,
Dressed in beauty, purpose and color,
Bestowed the gift of lighthearted flight.

Honeybees, too,
Acknowledged virtuosos of fast-moving song,
Play rhapsodic, dizzying concertos,
Always allegretto,

In honor of flower and queen –
Delectable honey,
Amber and sweet,
Their inimitable tribute and offering
To ordained and reigning royalty.

Symphonies of spring
In the grand concert halls
Of Nature and the soul,
Thrill ear and imagination,
Delight heart and mind,
Thought and being.
How good it is
That they are played,
Rhapsodically
And in the grandest of style,
Flawlessly,
Joyously,
Year after year,
In the rapturous key
And exquisite harmonies,
Of spring!

The Sea and the Gull

Surging sea of love,
You are my beloved!
Awestruck,
I wing the billowing waters
Of your surging love,
Fly the heaving, thundering waves
Of your grace and bounty!

O great sea!
You are my inspiration,
The wind beneath my wings,
The flowing waters that bestow every joy,
Provide all goodly sustenance!
From my flight,
The flapping of my wings,
Can be heard,
"For me,
O great sea!
No other beloved has there ever been
Or can ever be!"

O gull of soaring faithfulness!
My love for you
Is as the depth of my waters,
The expanse of my sea!
O lover of my every billowing wave
And shining sands!
How unfailing your matchless, skillful flight!
How untiring your attraction,

Devotion to my waters!
From all this,
How deep my love for you!
How moving the solicitude I feel for you!
How endearing your complete surrender
To my flowing, sometimes howling, winds!

Sea of love!
Sea of my every hope and dream!
Your uplifting words,
Carried upon wind and wave
And from the very depths of your being,
Bring encouragement, thankfulness and joy,
Yet,
How heavily they weigh upon the heart,
For I have never been,
Nor will ever be,
Worthy of such kindly sentiments,
For without you I am as naught!
Without you, how could I ever be!
O surging sea of love!
It is you that calls to the winds,
Commands the waters!
From you come forth
Lustrous pearls of wisdom and knowledge,
Wonderment and awe.
By your command
Coral reefs of wondrous beauty,
Seabed and boundless waters
Gently nurture all that moves and swims,
All that lives,
In your vast, endless waters.

O gull of love!
O lover of my might and power,
My mystery and inviolable ways,
The bounties I bestow!
How I love you so!
Should it please the One
Who creates the waters, sky and wind,
He Who gives you wing and flight,
We will journey
The surging seas of love's eternity
And the vast, spanless shores of time,
As one,
Lover and beloved,
And in this,
O lover of mine,
I will surge
And you will soar,
This our eternal rendezvous,
Rapturous tryst of sea, gull and shore.

In this is wisdom
From the ocean of boundless wisdom,
This ocean but a drop
In the sight of the One Who causes
Seas to surge and waves to rise,
Gulls to fly and gulls to soar,
He Whose might and power,
Boundless love and bounteous grace
Beget every sea,
Power every wave,
Birth every wind,
Permeate all creation.

The Sword of Thy Pen

A sword
To cleave the dark clouds of contention and strife,
Rend asunder
The skies of injustice and pride,
Leave them dumbfounded, exposed,
Fallen from the sky,
A mighty saber
To cut through the veils of heaven and hell –
These I see in the all-conquering,
Unfailing
Sword of Thy Pen.

A sword
To strike down falsehood,
Set free the sun of truth and moon of love,
Stars adorning the ethereal heavens of understanding –
A sword wielded by the Hand of God
To infuse being, order into space and time
That brilliant orbs of meaning emerge,
Gleam and glisten,
Shine forth upon the page,
Inscribe transcendence upon the heart –
Such is the indomitable power
Of Thy resplendent Sword of Wisdom.

To inscribe a momentous Book
Revealed in scripts of godly light,
A Book to ponder, take to heart, reflect upon
In the supernal skies of the spirit,

Mystic depths of the soul –
It is the Mother Book,
Supernal guide composed in splendor and glory
By the luminous, lightning bright
Sword of Thy Knowledge!

From the Sword of Thy Love
Waft the sweet-scented perfume of the rose of rapture,
The redolence of the hyacinth of adoration.
These flow through the garden of the heart,
Inspire songbirds of the soul to warble and coo.
Winds of holiness,
Enamored of their sweet savors,
Clutch them to their bosom,
Release them into the heavens
To perfume the heavenly breezes of eternity.

The Sword of Thy Pen
Perfumes in intoxicating spirituality
And transforming light
All who seek Thee,
Who open their hearts to Thee!
These beseech Thee by Thy beauty
And splendrous grace
To thrust into their throbbing,
Awaiting bosoms,
The dazzling Sword of Thy Glory,
That it indelibly inscribe
In the vernal, lush garden of the heart
Scripts of everlasting fealty
On the holy, outspread scrolls of Thy will,
The luminous pages of Thy pleasure,
The rapturous, unfading book

Of longing to enter Thy holy Court,
Attain Thy holy Presence!